WILLIAM SHAKESPEARE was born in Stratford-upon-Avon in April, 1564, and his birth is traditionally celebrated on April 23. The facts of his life, known from surviving documents, are sparse. He was one of eight children born to John Shakespeare, a merchant of some standing in his community. William probably went to the King's New School in Stratford, but he had no university education. In November 1582, at the age of eighteen, he married Anne Hathaway, eight years his senior, who was pregnant with their first child, Susanna. She was born on May 26, 1583. Twins, a boy, Hamnet (who would die at age eleven), and a girl, Judith, were born in 1585. By 1592 Shakespeare had gone to London, working as an actor and already known as a playwright. A rival dramatist, Robert Greene, referred to him as "an upstart crow, beautified with our feathers." Shakespeare became a principal shareholder and playwright of the successful acting troupe the Lord Chamberlain's men (later, under James I, called the King's men). In 1599 the Lord Chamberlain's men built and occupied the Globe Theatre in Southwark near the Thames River. Here many of Shakespeare's plays were performed by the most famous actors of his time, including Richard Burbage, Will Kempe, and Robert Armin. In addition to his 37 plays, Shakespeare had a hand in others, including *Sir Thomas More* and *The Two Noble Kinsmen*, and he wrote poems, including *Venus and Adonis* and *The Rape of Lucrece*. His 154 sonnets were published, probably without his authorization, in 1609. In 1611 or 1612 he gave up his lodgings in London and devoted more and more of his time to retirement in Stratford, though he continued writing such plays as *The Tempest* and *Henry VIII* until about 1613. He died on April 23, 1616, and was buried in Holy Trinity Church, Stratford. No collected edition of his plays was published during his lifetime, but in 1623 two members of his acting company, John Heminges and Henry Condell, published the great collection now called the First Folio.

**Bantam Shakespeare
The Complete Works—29 Volumes
Edited by David Bevington
With forewords by Joseph Papp on the plays**

The Poems: Venus and Adonis, The Rape of Lucrece, The
Phoenix and Turtle, A Lover's Complaint,
the Sonnets

Antony and Cleopatra	*The Merchant of Venice*
As You Like It	*A Midsummer Night's Dream*
The Comedy of Errors	*Much Ado about Nothing*
Hamlet	*Othello*
Henry IV, Part One	*Richard II*
Henry IV, Part Two	*Richard III*
Henry V	*Romeo and Juliet*
Julius Caesar	*The Taming of the Shrew*
King Lear	*The Tempest*
Macbeth	*Twelfth Night*

Together in one volume:

Henry VI, Parts One, Two, and Three
King John and Henry VIII
Measure for Measure, All's Well that Ends Well, and
Troilus and Cressida
Three Early Comedies: Love's Labor's Lost, The Two
Gentlemen of Verona, The Merry
Wives of Windsor
Three Classical Tragedies: Titus Andronicus, Timon
of Athens, Coriolanus
The Late Romances: Pericles, Cymbeline, The Winter's
Tale, The Tempest

Two collections:

Four Comedies: The Taming of the Shrew, A Midsummer
Night's Dream, The Merchant of Venice,
Twelfth Night
Four Tragedies: Hamlet, Othello, King Lear, Macbeth

William Shakespeare

THE MERCHANT OF VENICE

Edited by
David Bevington

David Scott Kastan,
James Hammersmith,
and Robert Kean Turner,
Associate Editors

With a Foreword by
Joseph Papp

BANTAM BOOKS
NEW YORK · TORONTO · LONDON · SYDNEY · AUCKLAND

THE MERCHANT OF VENICE
*A Bantam Book / published by arrangement
with Scott, Foresman and Company*

PRINTING HISTORY
*Scott, Foresman edition published / January 1980
Bantam edition, with newly edited text and substantially revised,
edited, and amplified notes, introductions, and other
materials, published / February 1988
Valuable advice on staging matters has been
provided by Richard Hosley.
Collations checked by Eric Rasmussen.
Additional editorial assistance by Claire McEachern.*

Library of Congress Cataloging-in-Publication Data

Shakespeare, William, 1564–1616.
    The merchant of Venice / William Shakespeare; edited by David
Bevington; David Scott Kastan, James Hammersmith, and Robert Kean
Turner, associate editors; with a foreword by Joseph Papp.
    p.   cm.—(A Bantam classic)
    "Bantam edition with newly edited text and substantially revised,
edited, and amplified notes, introductions, and other materials"—
—T.p. verso.
    Bibliography: p.
    ISBN 0-553-21299-0 (pbk.)
    I. Bevington, David M.   II. Title.
PR2825.A2B45   1988
822.3'3—dc19   87-24088
                                                                CIP

Published simultaneously in the United States and Canada

PRINTED IN THE UNITED STATES OF AMERICA

O   0 9 8 7 6 5 4

Contents

THE MERCHANT OF VENICE

Foreword

It's hard to imagine, but Shakespeare wrote all of his plays with a quill pen, a goose feather whose hard end had to be sharpened frequently. How many times did he scrape the dull end to a point with his knife, dip it into the inkwell, and bring up, dripping wet, those wonderful words and ideas that are known all over the world?

In the age of word processors, typewriters, and ballpoint pens, we have almost forgotten the meaning of the word "blot." Yet when I went to school, in the 1930s, my classmates and I knew all too well what an inkblot from the metal-tipped pens we used would do to a nice clean page of a test paper, and we groaned whenever a splotch fell across the sheet. Most of us finished the school day with ink-stained fingers; those who were less careful also went home with ink-stained shirts, which were almost impossible to get clean.

When I think about how long it took me to write the simplest composition with a metal-tipped pen and ink, I can only marvel at how many plays Shakespeare scratched out with his goose-feather quill pen, year after year. Imagine him walking down one of the narrow cobblestoned streets of London, or perhaps drinking a pint of beer in his local alehouse. Suddenly his mind catches fire with an idea, or a sentence, or a previously elusive phrase. He is burning with impatience to write it down—but because he doesn't have a ballpoint pen or even a pencil in his pocket, he has to keep the idea in his head until he can get to his quill and parchment.

He rushes back to his lodgings on Silver Street, ignoring the vendors hawking brooms, the coaches clattering by, the piteous wails of beggars and prisoners. Bounding up the stairs, he snatches his quill and starts to write furiously, not even bothering to light a candle against the dusk. "To be, or not to be," he scrawls, "that is the—." But the quill point has gone dull, the letters have fattened out illegibly, and in the middle of writing one of the most famous passages in the history of dramatic literature, Shakespeare has to stop to sharpen his pen.

Taking a deep breath, he lights a candle now that it's dark, sits down, and begins again. By the time the candle has burned out and the noisy apprentices of his French Huguenot landlord have quieted down, Shakespeare has finished Act 3 of *Hamlet* with scarcely a blot.

Early the next morning, he hurries through the fog of a London summer morning to the rooms of his colleague Richard Burbage, the actor for whom the role of Hamlet is being written. He finds Burbage asleep and snoring loudly, sprawled across his straw mattress. Not only had the actor performed in *Henry V* the previous afternoon, but he had then gone out carousing all night with some friends who had come to the performance.

Shakespeare shakes his friend awake, until, bleary-eyed, Burbage sits up in his bed. "Dammit, Will," he grumbles, "can't you let an honest man sleep?" But the playwright, his eyes shining and the words tumbling out of his mouth, says, "Shut up and listen—tell me what you think of *this*!"

He begins to read to the still half-asleep Burbage, pacing around the room as he speaks. ". . . Whether 'tis nobler in the mind to suffer the slings and arrows of outrageous fortune—"

Burbage interrupts, suddenly wide awake, "That's excellent, very good, 'the slings and arrows of outrageous fortune,' yes, I think it will work quite well. . . ." He takes the parchment from Shakespeare and murmurs the lines to himself, slowly at first but with growing excitement.

The sun is just coming up, and the words of one of Shakespeare's most famous soliloquies are being uttered for the first time by the first actor ever to bring Hamlet to life. It must have been an exhilarating moment.

Shakespeare wrote most of his plays to be performed live by the actor Richard Burbage and the rest of the Lord Chamberlain's men (later the King's men). Today, however, our first encounter with the plays is usually in the form of the printed word. And there is no question that reading Shakespeare for the first time isn't easy. His plays aren't comic books or magazines or the dime-store detective novels I read when I was young. A lot of his sentences are complex. Many of his words are no longer used in our everyday

speech. His profound thoughts are often condensed into poetry, which is not as straightforward as prose.

Yet when you hear the words spoken aloud, a lot of the
language may strike you as unexpectedly modern. For
Shakespeare's plays, like any dramatic work, weren't really
meant to be read; they were meant to be spoken, seen, and
performed. It's amazing how lines that are so troublesome
in print can flow so naturally and easily when spoken.

I think it was precisely this music that first fascinated
me. When I was growing up, Shakespeare was a stranger to
me. I had no particular interest in him, for I was from a
different cultural tradition. It never occurred to me that his
plays might be more than just something to "get through"
in school, like science or math or the physical education
requirement we had to fulfill. My passions then were
movies, radio, and vaudeville—certainly not Elizabethan
drama.

I was, however, fascinated by words and language. Because I grew up in a home where Yiddish was spoken, and
English was only a second language, I was acutely sensitive
to the musical sounds of different languages and had an ear
for lilt and cadence and rhythm in the spoken word. And so
I loved reciting poems and speeches even as a very young
child. In first grade I learned lots of short nature verses—
"Who has seen the wind?," one of them began. My first
foray into drama was playing the role of Scrooge in Charles
Dickens's *A Christmas Carol* when I was eight years old. I
liked summoning all the scorn and coldness I possessed and
putting them into the words, "Bah, humbug!"

From there I moved on to longer and more famous poems
and other works by writers of the 1930s. Then, in junior
high school, I made my first acquaintance with Shakespeare through his play *Julius Caesar*. Our teacher, Miss
McKay, assigned the class a passage to memorize from the
opening scene of the play, the one that begins "Wherefore
rejoice? What conquest brings he home?" The passage
seemed so wonderfully theatrical and alive to me, and the
experience of memorizing and reciting it was so much fun,
that I went on to memorize another speech from the play on
my own.

I chose Mark Antony's address to the crowd in Act 3,

scene 2, which struck me then as incredibly high drama.
Even today, when I speak the words, I feel the same thrill I
did that first time. There is the strong and athletic Antony
descending from the raised pulpit where he has been speaking, right into the midst of a crowded Roman square. Hold-
ing the torn and bloody cloak of the murdered Julius
Caesar in his hand, he begins to speak to the people of
Rome:

> If you have tears, prepare to shed them now.
> You all do know this mantle. I remember
> The first time ever Caesar put it on;
> 'Twas on a summer's evening in his tent,
> That day he overcame the Nervii.
> Look, in this place ran Cassius' dagger through.
> See what a rent the envious Casca made.
> Through this the well-belovèd Brutus stabbed,
> And as he plucked his cursèd steel away,
> Mark how the blood of Caesar followed it,
> As rushing out of doors to be resolved
> If Brutus so unkindly knocked or no;
> For Brutus, as you know, was Caesar's angel.
> Judge, O you gods, how dearly Caesar loved him!
> This was the most unkindest cut of all . . .

I'm not sure now that I even knew Shakespeare had written a lot of other plays, or that he was considered "time-
less," "universal," or "classic"—but I knew a good speech
when I heard one, and I found the splendid rhythms of
Antony's rhetoric as exciting as anything I'd ever come
across.

Fifty years later, I still feel that way. Hearing good actors
speak Shakespeare gracefully and naturally is a wonderful
experience, unlike any other I know. There's a satisfying
fullness to the spoken word that the printed page just can't
convey. This is why seeing the plays of Shakespeare performed live in a theater is the best way to appreciate them.
If you can't do that, listening to sound recordings or watching film versions of the plays is the next best thing.

But if you do start with the printed word, use the play as a
script. Be an actor yourself and say the lines out loud. Don't
worry too much at first about words you don't immediately
understand. Look them up in the footnotes or a dictionary,

but don't spend too much time on this. It is more profitable (and fun) to get the sense of a passage and sing it out. Speak naturally, almost as if you were talking to a friend, but be sure to enunciate the words properly. You'll be surprised at how much you understand simply by speaking the speech "trippingly on the tongue," as Hamlet advises the Players.

You might start, as I once did, with a speech from *Julius Caesar*, in which the tribune (city official) Marullus scolds the commoners for transferring their loyalties so quickly from the defeated and murdered general Pompey to the newly victorious Julius Caesar:

> Wherefore rejoice? What conquest brings he home?
> What tributaries follow him to Rome
> To grace in captive bonds his chariot wheels?
> You blocks, you stones, you worse than senseless
>   things!
> O you hard hearts, you cruel men of Rome,
> Knew you not Pompey? Many a time and oft
> Have you climbed up to walls and battlements,
> To towers and windows, yea, to chimney tops,
> Your infants in your arms, and there have sat
> The livelong day, with patient expectation,
> To see great Pompey pass the streets of Rome.

With the exception of one or two words like "wherefore" (which means "why," not "where"), "tributaries" (which means "captives"), and "patient expectation" (which means patient waiting), the meaning and emotions of this speech can be easily understood.

From here you can go on to dialogues or other more challenging scenes. Although you may stumble over unaccustomed phrases or unfamiliar words at first, and even fall flat when you're crossing some particularly rocky passages, pick yourself up and stay with it. Remember that it takes time to feel at home with anything new. Soon you'll come to recognize Shakespeare's unique sense of humor and way of saying things as easily as you recognize a friend's laughter.

And then it will just be a matter of choosing which one of Shakespeare's plays you want to tackle next. As a true fan of his, you'll find that you're constantly learning from his plays. It's a journey of discovery that you can continue for

the rest of your life. For no matter how many times you read
or see a particular play, there will always be something new
there that you won't have noticed before.

Why do so many thousands of people get hooked on
Shakespeare and develop a habit that lasts a lifetime? What
can he really say to us today, in a world filled with inven-
tions and problems he never could have imagined? And how
do you get past his special language and difficult sentence
structure to understand him?

The best way to answer these questions is to go see a live
production. You might not know much about Shakespeare,
or much about the theater, but when you watch actors performing one of his plays on the stage, it will soon become
clear to you why people get so excited about a playwright
who lived hundreds of years ago.

For the story—what's happening in the play—is the most
accessible part of Shakespeare. In *A Midsummer Night's
Dream*, for example, you can immediately understand the
situation: a girl is chasing a guy who's chasing a girl who's
chasing another guy. No wonder *A Midsummer Night's
Dream* is one of the most popular of Shakespeare's plays:
it's about one of the world's most popular pastimes—
falling in love.

But the course of true love never did run smooth, as the
young suitor Lysander says. Often in Shakespeare's comedies the girl whom the guy loves doesn't love him back, or
she loves him but he loves someone else. In *The Two Gentlemen of Verona*, Julia loves Proteus, Proteus loves Sylvia,
and Sylvia loves Valentine, who is Proteus's best friend. In
the end, of course, true love prevails, but not without lots of
complications along the way.

For in all of his plays—comedies, histories, and tragedies—Shakespeare is showing you human nature. His characters act and react in the most extraordinary ways—and
sometimes in the most incomprehensible ways. People are
always trying to find motivations for what a character does.
They ask, "Why does Iago want to destroy Othello?"

The answer, to me, is very simple—because that's the way
Iago is. That's just his nature. Shakespeare doesn't explain
his characters; he sets them in motion—and away they go.
He doesn't worry about whether they're likable or not. He's

interested in interesting people, and his most fascinating characters are those who are unpredictable. If you lean back in your chair early on in one of his plays, thinking you've figured out what Iago or Shylock (in *The Merchant of Venice*) is up to, don't be too sure—because that great judge of human nature, Shakespeare, will surprise you every time.

He is just as wily in the way he structures a play. In *Macbeth*, a comic scene is suddenly introduced just after the bloodiest and most treacherous slaughter imaginable, of a guest and king by his host and subject, when in comes a drunk porter who has to go to the bathroom. Shakespeare is tickling your emotions by bringing a stand-up comic on-stage right on the heels of a savage murder.

It has taken me thirty years to understand even some of these things, and so I'm not suggesting that Shakespeare is immediately understandable. I've gotten to know him not through theory but through practice, the practice of the *living* Shakespeare—the playwright of the theater.

Of course the plays are a great achievement of dramatic literature, and they should be studied and analyzed in schools and universities. But you must always remember, when reading all the words *about* the playwright and his plays, that *Shakespeare's* words came first and that in the end there is nothing greater than a single actor on the stage speaking the lines of Shakespeare.

Everything important that I know about Shakespeare comes from the practical business of producing and directing his plays in the theater. The task of classifying, criticizing, and editing Shakespeare's printed works I happily leave to others. For me, his plays really do live on the stage, not on the page. That is what he wrote them for and that is how they are best appreciated.

Although Shakespeare lived and wrote hundreds of years ago, his name rolls off my tongue as if he were my brother. As a producer and director, I feel that there is a professional relationship between us that spans the centuries. As a human being, I feel that Shakespeare has enriched my understanding of life immeasurably. I hope you'll let him do the same for you.

❧

The Merchant of Venice has been one of Shakespeare's most popular—and controversial—plays wherever it has been performed. The controversy usually centers around the way Shylock the Jew is portrayed and treated. Many people think that Shakespeare himself was being anti-Semitic here. I personally don't believe this, judging from the humanity in all the works of this great writer, especially this one. It's difficult for me to label *The Merchant of Venice* as anti-Semitic when it has one of the most eloquent pleas to our sense of common humanity ever uttered on the stage:

> Hath not a Jew eyes? Hath not a Jew hands, organs, dimensions, senses, affections, passions? Fed with the same food, hurt with the same weapons, subject to the same diseases, healed by the same means, warmed and cooled by the same winter and summer, as a Christian is? If you prick us, do we not bleed? If you tickle us, do we not laugh? If you poison us, do we not die? And if you wrong us, shall we not revenge?

There is no indication that the romantic lead, Bassanio, and the woman he marries, Portia, are prejudiced against Shylock because he's a Jew. Portia's goal is to save Antonio's life in order to free her new husband from his obligations to the merchant. Bassanio wants to rescue a friend to whom he's heavily indebted. It would be difficult to prove that anything either of them says has an unusually anti-Semitic prejudice.

And yet there is anti-Semitism *within* the play. We find it most virulently in Antonio, the merchant of Venice, and his henchmen Salerio and Solanio, very strongly in Gratiano, somewhat in Lorenzo, and especially in the comedian Launcelot Gobbo, Shylock's former servant.

The Merchant of Venice was the first play we at the New York Shakespeare Festival produced at the Delacorte Theater in Central Park, with George C. Scott as Shylock. I can remember telling George not to play for sympathy, not to be nice, not to turn the other cheek, but to feel the righteous anger that belongs to him. After all, Shylock has been so kicked around and spat on just for trying to make a living that it would be unnatural for him *not* to want vengeance. He's taunted in the streets; his daughter runs away with a

Christian, taking his money and jewels with her; the ruling elite in Venice, personified by Antonio, are arrayed against him—who wouldn't press for his pound of flesh in those circumstances?

Shakespeare provides Shylock with a rationale—but not an excuse—for his behavior. But Antonio, unlike Shylock, has no real reason for his hatred and cruelty toward the Jewish man; nor can there ever be a rational explanation for anti-Semitism. Antonio treats Shylock abominably. In the early scenes of the play we learn that he has spurned and spat upon him, calling him a dog, and Antonio goes on to say, "I am as like to call thee so again, To spit on thee again, to spurn thee too." In the trial scene, Shylock is threatened with the confiscation of all of his remaining money and property. The compromise suggested by Antonio requires, among other things, that Shylock change his religion—the cruelest punishment that could be devised.

One of the most poignant moments Shakespeare gives Shylock occurs when Tubal tells him that Jessica, Shylock's daughter, who has run off with Lorenzo, has traded a family ring for a monkey. "It was my turquoise," says Shylock, "I had it of Leah when I was a bachelor. I would not have given it for a wilderness of monkeys." What makes me sad here is that Jessica seems to have completely disregarded the emotional value of the ring. There seems to be very little triumph in her act; instead, Jessica must suffer the consequences of her actions, as we perceive in the last scenes of the play, where she is unaccountably melancholic.

Because of Shylock, *The Merchant of Venice* can easily be called a tragedy. He will always remain a complex, fascinating character. No wonder so many actors want to play him, to understand him, and to enter into his tragedy—he is one of the greatest dramatic figures of all time.

JOSEPH PAPP

JOSEPH PAPP GRATEFULLY ACKNOWLEDGES THE HELP OF ELIZABETH KIRKLAND IN PREPARING THIS FOREWORD.

Introduction

Although Shylock is the most prominent character in *The Merchant of Venice*, he takes part in neither the beginning nor the ending of the play. Nor is he the "merchant" of the title, but a moneylender whose usury is portrayed as the very opposite of true commerce. His vengeful struggle to obtain a pound of flesh from Antonio contrasts with the various romantic episodes woven together in this play: Bassanio's choosing of Portia by means of the caskets, Gratiano's wooing of Nerissa, Jessica's elopement with Lorenzo, Launcelot Gobbo's changing of masters, and the episode of the rings. In all these stories, friendship and love triumph over faithlessness and hatred. However much we may come to sympathize with Shylock's misfortunes and question the motives of his enemies, however much we are made uncomfortable by the potential insularity of a Venetian ethic that has no genuine place for non-Christians or cultural outsiders, Shylock remains essentially the villain of a love comedy. His remorseless pursuit of Antonio darkens the mood of the play, and his overthrow signals the providential triumph of love and friendship, even though that triumph is not without its undercurrent of wry melancholy. Before we examine the undoubted ironies of his situation more closely, we need to establish the structural context of this love comedy as a whole.

Like many of Shakespeare's philosophical and festive comedies, *The Merchant of Venice* presents two contrasting worlds, one idealized and the other marked by conflict and anxiety. To an extent, these contrasting worlds can be identified with the locations of Belmont and Venice. Belmont, to which the various happy lovers and their friends eventually retire, is a place of magic and love. As its name implies, it is on a mountain, and it is reached by a journey across water. It is pure, serene, ethereal. As often happens in fairy stories, on this mountain dwells a princess who must be won by means of a riddling contest. We usually see Belmont at night. Music surrounds it, and women preside over it. Even its caskets, houses, and rings are essentially feminine symbols. Venice, on the other hand, is a place of bustle and economic competition, seen most characteristically in the heat of the day. It lies low and flat, at a point where rivers reach the sea. Men preside over its contentious marketplace and its haggling law courts. Actually, the opposition of Venice and Belmont is not quite so clear-cut: Venice contains much compassionate friendship, whereas Belmont is subject to the arbitrary command of Portia's dead father. (Portia somewhat resembles Jessica in being imprisoned by her father's will.) Even though Portia descends to Venice in the angelic role of mercy-giver, she also remains very human: sharp-tongued and even venomous in caricaturing her unwelcome wooers, crafty in her legal maneuvering, saucily prankish in her torturing of Bassanio about the rings. Nevertheless the polarity of two contrasting localities and two groups of characters is vividly real in this play.

The play's opening scene, from which Shylock is excluded, sets forth the interrelated themes of friendship, romantic love, and risk, or "hazard." The merchant of the title, Antonio, is the victim of a mysterious melancholy. He is wealthy enough and surrounded by friends, but something is missing from his life. He assures his solicitous companions that he has no financial worries, for he has been too careful to trust all his cargoes to one sea vessel. Antonio in fact has no idea why he is so sad. The question is haunting: what is the matter? Perhaps the answer is to be found in a paradox: those who strive to prosper in the world's terms are doomed to frustration, not because prosperity will necessarily elude them but because it will not satisfy the spirit. "You have too much respect upon the world," argues the carefree Gratiano. "They lose it that do buy it with much care" (1.1.74–75). Portia and Jessica too are at first afflicted by a melancholy that stems from the incompleteness of living isolated lives, with insufficient opportunities for love and sacrifice. They must learn, as Antonio learns with the help of his dear friend Bassanio, to seek happiness by daring to risk everything for friendship. Antonio's risk is most extreme: only when he has thrown away concern for his life can he discover what there is to live for.

At first, Bassanio's request for assistance seems just as materialistic as the worldliness from which Antonio suffers. Bassanio proposes to marry a rich young lady, Portia, in order to recoup his fortune lost through prodigality, and he needs money from Antonio so that he may woo Portia in proper fashion. She is "richly left," the heiress of a dead father, a golden fleece for whom this new Jason will make a quest. Bassanio's adventure is partly commercial. Yet his pilgrimage for Portia is magnanimous as well. The occasional modern practice of playing Bassanio and Portia as cynical antiheroes of a "black" comedy points up the problematic character of their materialism and calculation, but it inevitably distorts the play. Bassanio has lost his previous fortune through the amiable faults of reckless generosity and a lack of concern for financial prudence. The money he must now borrow, and the fortune he hopes to acquire, are to him no more than a means to carefree happiness. Although Portia's rich dowry is a strong consideration, he describes her also as "fair, and fairer than that word, / Of wondrous virtues" (1.1.162–163). Moreover, he enjoys the element of risk in wooing her. It is like shooting a second arrow in order to recover one that has been lost—double or nothing. This gamble, or "hazard," involves risk for Antonio as well as for Bassanio, and ultimately brings a double reward to them both, spiritual as well as financial. Unless one recognizes these aspects of Bassanio's quest, as well as the clear fairy-tale quality with which Shakespeare deliberately invests this part of the plot, one cannot properly assess Bassanio's role in this romantic comedy.

Bassanio's quest for Portia can in fact never succeed until he disavows the very financial considerations that brought him to Belmont in the first place. This is the paradox of the riddle of the three caskets, an ancient parable stressing the need for choosing by true substance rather than by outward show. To choose "what many men desire," as the Prince of Morocco does, is to pin one's hopes on worldly wealth; to believe that one "deserves" good fortune, as the Prince of Aragon does, is to reveal a fatal pride in one's own merit. Bassanio perceives that in order to win true love he must "give and hazard all he hath." He is not "deceived with ornament" (3.2.74). Just as Antonio must risk all for friendship, and just as Bassanio himself must later be willing to risk losing Portia for the higher cause of true friendship (in the episode of the rings), Bassanio must renounce worldly ambition and beauty before he can be rewarded with success. Paradoxically, only those who learn to subdue such worldly desires may then legitimately enjoy the world's pleasures. Only they have acknowledged the hierarchical subservience of the flesh to the spirit. These are the philosophical truisms of Renaissance Neoplatonism, depicting love as a chain or ladder from the basest carnality to the supreme love of God for man. On this ladder, perfect friendship and spiritual union are more sublimely Godlike than sexual fulfillment. This idealism may seem a strange doctrine for Bassanio the fortune hunter, but actually its conventional wisdom simply confirms his role as romantic hero. He and Portia are not denied worldly happiness or erotic pleasure; they are merely asked to give first thought to their Christian duty in marriage. The essentially Christian paradox of losing the world in order to gain the world lies at the center of their love relationship. This paradox illuminates not only the casket episode but the struggle for the pound of flesh, the elopement of Jessica, the ring episode, and even the comic foolery of Launcelot Gobbo.

Shylock, in his quest for the pound of flesh, represents a denial of all the paradoxical Christian truths just described. As a usurer he refuses to lend money interest-free in the name of friendship. Instead of taking risks, he insists on his bond. He spurns mercy and demands strict justice. By calculating all his chances too craftily, he appears to win at first but must eventually lose all. He has "too much respect upon the world" (1.1.74). His God is the Old Testament God of Moses, the God of wrath, the God of the Ten Commandments with their forbidding emphasis on "Thou shalt not." (This oversimplified contrast between Judaism and Christianity was commonplace in Shakespeare's time.) Shylock abhors stealing but admires equivocation as a means of outmaneuvering a competitor; he approvingly cites Jacob's ruse to deprive Laban of his sheep (1.3.69–88). Any tactic is permissible so long as it falls within the realm of legality and contract.

Shylock's ethical outlook, then, justifies both usury and the old dispensation of the Jewish law. The two are philosophically combined, just as usury and Judaism had become equated in the popular imagination of Renaissance Europe. Even though lending at interest was becoming increasingly necessary and common, old prejudices against it still persisted. Angry moralists pointed out that the New Testament had condemned usury and that Aristotle had described money as barren. To breed money was therefore regarded as unnatural. Usury was considered sinful because it did not involve the usual risks of commerce; the lender was assured against loss of his principal by the posting of collateral and, at the same time, was sure to earn a handsome interest. The usurer seemed to be getting something for nothing. For these reasons usury was sometimes declared illegal. Its practitioners were viewed as corrupt and grasping, hated as misers. In some European countries, Jews were permitted to practice this un-Christian living (and permitted to do very little else) and then, hypocritically, were detested for performing un-Christian deeds. Ironically, the moneylenders of England were Christians, and few Jews were to be found in any professions. Nominally excluded since Edward I's reign, the Jews had returned in small numbers to London but did not practice their Judaism openly. They attended Anglican services as required by law and then worshiped in private, relatively undisturbed by the authorities. Shylock is not based on observation from London life. He is derived from continental tradition and reflects a widespread conviction that Jews and usurers were alike in being non-Christian and sinister.

Shylock is unquestionably sinister. On the Elizabethan stage the actor portraying him apparently wore a red beard, as in traditional representations of Judas, and a hooked nose. He bears an "ancient grudge" against Antonio simply because Antonio is "a Christian." We recognize in Shylock the archetype of the supposed Jew who wishes to kill a Christian and obtain his flesh. In early medieval anti-Semitic legends of this sort, the flesh thus obtained was imagined to be eaten ritually during Passover. Because some Jews had once persecuted Christ, all were unfairly presumed to be implacable enemies of all Christians. These anti-Semitic superstitions were likely to erupt into hysteria at any time, as in 1594 when Dr. Roderigo Lopez, a Portuguese Jewish physician, was accused of having plotted against the life of Queen Elizabeth and of Don Antonio, pretender to the Portuguese throne. Marlowe's *The Jew of Malta* was revived for this occasion, enjoying an unusually successful run of fifteen performances, and scholars have often wondered if Shakespeare's play was not written under the same impetus. On this score the evidence is inconclusive, and the play might have been written any time between 1594 and 1598 (when it is mentioned by Francis Meres in his *Palladis Tamia*), but in any case Shakespeare has made no attempt to avoid the anti-Semitic nature of his story.

To offset the portrayal of Jewish villainy, however, the play also dramatizes the possibility of conversion to Christianity, suggesting that Judaism is more a matter of benighted faith than of ethnic origin. Converted Jews were not new on the stage: they had appeared in medieval cycle drama, in the Croxton *Play of the Sacrament* (late fifteenth century), and more recently in *The Jew of Malta*, in which Barabas's daughter Abigail falls in love with a Christian and eventually becomes a nun. Shylock's daughter Jessica similarly embraces Christianity as Lorenzo's wife and is received into the happy comradeship of Belmont. Shylock is forced to accept Christianity, presumably for the benefit of his eternal soul. Earlier in the play, Antonio repeatedly indicates his willingness to befriend Shylock if the latter will only give up usury, and is even cautiously hopeful when Shylock offers him an interest-free loan: "The Hebrew will turn Christian; he grows kind" (1.3.177). To be sure, Antonio's denunciation of Shylock's usurious Judaism has been vehement and personal; we learn that he has spat on Shylock's gaberdine and kicked him as one would kick a dog. This violent disapproval offers no opportunity for the toleration of cultural and religious differences that we expect today from persons of good will, but at least Antonio is prepared to accept Shylock if Shylock will embrace the Christian faith and its ethical responsibilities. Whether the play itself endorses Antonio's Christian point of view as normative, or insists on a darker reading by making us uneasy with intolerance, is a matter of unceasing critical debate. Quite possibly, the play's power to disturb emanates at least in part from the dramatic conflict of irreconcilable sets of values.

To Antonio, then, as well as to other Venetians, true Christianity is both an absolute good from which no deviation is possible without evil, and a state of faith to which aliens

may turn by abjuring the benighted creeds of their ances-
tors. By this token, the Prince of Morocco is condemned to
failure in his quest for Portia not so much because he is
black as because he is an infidel, one who worships "blind
fortune" and therefore chooses a worldly rather than a spiritual reward. Although Portia pertly dismisses him with
"Let all of his complexion choose me so" (2.7.79), she pro-
fesses earlier to find him handsome and agrees that he
should not be judged by his complexion (2.1.13–22). Unless
she is merely being hypocritical, she means by her later remark that black-skinned men are generally infidels, just as
Jews are as a group non-Christian. Such pejorative thinking
about persons as types is no doubt distressing and suggests
at least to a modern audience the cultural limitation of Portia's view, but in any case it shows her to be no less well-
disposed toward blacks than toward others who are also
alien. She rejects the Prince of Aragon because he too lacks
proper faith, though nominally a Christian. All human be-
ings, therefore, may aspire to truly virtuous conduct, and
those who choose virtue are equally blessed; but the terms
of defining that ideal are essentially Christian. Jews and
blacks may rise spiritually only by abandoning their pagan
creeds for the new dispensation of charity and forgiveness.

The superiority of Christian teaching to the older Jewish
dispensation was of course a widely accepted notion of
Shakespeare's time. After all, these were the years when
men fought and died to maintain their religious beliefs. Today the notion of a single true church is less widely held,
and we have difficulty understanding why anyone would
wish to force conversion on Shylock. Modern productions
find it tempting to portray Shylock as a victim of bigotry,
and to put great stress on his heartrending assertions of his
humanity: "Hath not a Jew eyes? . . . If you prick us, do we
not bleed?" (3.1.55–61). Shylock does indeed suffer from his
enemies, and his sufferings add a tortured complexity to
this play—even, one suspects, for an Elizabethan audience.
Those who profess Christianity must surely examine their
own motives and conduct. Is it right to steal treasure from
Shylock's house along with his eloped daughter? Is it con-
siderate of Jessica and Lorenzo to squander Shylock's turquoise ring, the gift of his wife, Leah, on a monkey? Does
Shylock's vengeful insistence on law justify the quibbling

countermeasures devised by Portia even as she piously declaims about mercy? Do Shylock's misfortunes deserve the mirthful parodies of Solanio ("My daughter! O my ducats!") or the hostile jeering of Gratiano at the conclusion of the trial? Because he stands outside Christian faith, Shylock can provide a perspective whereby we see the hypocrisies of those who profess a higher ethical code. Nevertheless, Shylock's compulsive desire for vengeance according to an Old Testament code of an eye for an eye cannot be justified by the wrongdoings of any particular Christian. Such deeds condemn the doer rather than undermine the Christian standards of true virtue as ideally expressed. Shakespeare humanizes Shylock by portraying him as a believable and sensitive man, and shows much that is to be regretted in Shylock's Christian antagonists, but he also allows Shylock to place himself in the wrong by his refusal to forgive his enemies.

Shylock thus loses everything through his effort to win everything on his own terms. His daughter, Jessica, by her elopement, follows an opposite course. She characterizes her father's home as "hell," and she resents being locked up behind closed windows. Shylock detests music and the sounds of merriment; Jessica's new life in Belmont is immersed in music. He is old, suspicious, miserly; she is young, loving, adventurous. Most important, she seems to be at least part Christian when we first see her. As Launcelot jests half in earnest, "If a Christian did not play the knave and get thee, I am much deceived" (2.3.11–12). Her removal from Shylock's house involves theft, and her running from Venice is, she confesses, an "unthrift love." Paradoxically, however, she sees this recklessness as of more blessed effect than her father's legalistic caution. As she says, "I shall be saved by my husband. He hath made me a Christian" (3.5.17–18).

Launcelot Gobbo's clowning offers a similarly paradoxical comment on the tragedy of Shylock. Launcelot's debate with himself about whether or not to leave Shylock's service is put in terms of a soul struggle between his conscience and the devil (2.2.1–29). Conscience bids him stay, for service is a debt, a bond, an obligation, whereas abandonment of one's indenture is a kind of rebellion or stealing away. Yet Shylock's house is "hell" to Launcelot as to Jessica. Comparing his new master with his old, Launcelot observes to Bassanio, "you have the grace of God, sir, and he hath enough" (142–143). Service with Bassanio involves imprudent risks, since Bassanio is a spendthrift. The miserly Shylock rejoices to see the ever hungry Launcelot, this "huge feeder," wasting the substance of a hated Christian. Once again, however, Shylock will lose everything in his grasping quest for security. Another spiritual renewal occurs when Launcelot encounters his old and nearly blind father (2.2). In a scene echoing the biblical stories of the Prodigal Son and of Jacob and Esau, Launcelot teases the old man with false rumors of Launcelot's own death in order to make their reunion seem all the more unexpected and precious. The illusion of loss gives way to joy: Launcelot is, in language adapted from the liturgy, "your boy that was, your son that is, your child that shall be" (81–82).

In the episode of the rings we encounter a final playful variation on the paradox of winning through losing. Portia and Nerissa cleverly present their new husbands with a cruel choice: disguised as a doctor of laws and his clerk, who have just saved the life of Antonio from Shylock's wrath, the two wives ask nothing more for their services than the rings they see on the fingers of Bassanio and Gratiano. The two husbands, who have vowed never to part with these wedding rings, must therefore choose between love and friendship. The superior claim of friendship is clear, no matter what the cost, and Portia knows well enough that Bassanio's obedience to this Neoplatonic ideal is an essential part of his virtue. Just as he previously renounced beauty and riches before he could deserve Portia, he must now risk losing her for friendship's sake. The testing of the husbands' constancy does border at times on gratuitous harshness and exercise of power, for it deals with the oldest of masculine nightmares, cuckoldry. Wives are not without weapons in the struggle for control in marriage, and Portia and Nerissa enjoy trapping their new husbands in a no-win situation. Still, the threat is easily resolved by the dispelling of farcically mistaken identities. The young men have been tricked into bestowing their rings on their wives for a second time in the name of perfect friendship, thereby confirming a relationship that is both Platonic and fleshly. As Gratiano bawdily points out in the play's last line, the ring is both a spiritual and a sexual symbol of marriage. The resolution of this illusory quarrel also brings to an end the merry battle of the sexes between wives and husbands. Having hinted at the sorts of misunderstandings that afflict even the best of human relationships, and having proved themselves wittily able to torture and deceive their husbands, Portia and Nerissa submit at last to the authority of Bassanio and Gratiano.

All appears to be in harmony in Belmont. The disorders of Venice have been left far behind, however imperfectly they may have been resolved. Jessica and Lorenzo contrast their present happiness with the sufferings of less fortunate lovers of long ago: Troilus and Cressida, Pyramus and Thisbe, Aeneas and Dido, Jason and Medea. The tranquil joy found in Belmont is attuned to the music of the spheres, the singing of the "young-eyed cherubins" (5.1.62), although with a proper Christian humility the lovers also realize that the harmony of immortal souls is infinitely beyond their comprehension. Bound in by the grossness of the flesh, "this muddy vesture of decay" (5.1.64), they can only reach toward the bliss of eternity through music and the perfect friendship of true love. Even in their final joy, accordingly, the lovers find an incompleteness that lends a wistful and slightly melancholy reflective tone to the play's ending; but this Christian sense of the unavoidable incompleteness of all human life is of a very different order from that earlier melancholy of isolation and lack of commitment experienced by Portia, Jessica, Antonio, and others.

The Merchant of Venice
in Performance

"Shylock is a bloody-minded monster," confided Henry Irving in 1879, "but you mustn't play him so, if you wish to succeed; you must get some sympathy with him." The paradox that Irving described is central to the history of *The Merchant of Venice* in performance. Shylock is the play's villain, but he is also a towering presence onstage. Actors who have undertaken the role of Shylock have seldom been content (since the early eighteenth century, at any rate) to see him as simply a villain to be jeered at and cast out; instead, they have been drawn toward a tragic interpretation, sometimes so much so that the rest of the play has suffered.

In the first century and a half of its stage history, *The Merchant of Venice* was not often staged at all, possibly because audiences were not yet ready for a sympathetic Shylock. Shakespeare's acting company, the Lord Chamberlain's men, performed the play "divers times" before 1600 and (now called the King's men) twice at court in February of 1605, and they probably played it in a comic vein of acting (with Richard Burbage as Shylock in a red wig, according to a doubtful tradition), though one would like to think that the original performances also found room for a complex and even troubled response. For a long while thereafter, the play virtually disappeared from the stage. Thomas Betterton took the role not of Shylock but of Bassanio in an adaptation called *The Jew of Venice*, by George Granville, Lord Lansdowne, at the theater in Lincoln's Inn Fields, London, in 1701. Despite its title, this heavily rearranged version reduced the importance of Shylock in order both to ennoble the role of Bassanio and to provide the kind of masquelike spectacle demanded by Restoration audiences. The play opens on a banquet given by Bassanio, at which Antonio proposes a toast to eternal friendship; Bassanio, one to love; Gratiano, to women; and Shylock, sitting apart, to money. The banquet concludes with a long masque of Peleus and Thetis. In an added prison scene, Shylock protests to Antonio that he will have his bond. During the trial scene, Gratiano is given a number of interpolated lines to augment the comedy of his attack on Shylock. Shylock's rage against his daughter's elopement is toned down, and he is not forced to convert to Christianity. The Gobbos have disappeared. Thomas Doggett, the actor who played Shylock, was renowned as a comic actor and may have modeled his performance on disreputable moneylenders of his own day. Granville's version persisted well into the eighteenth century, though sometimes without the masque.

Charles Macklin not only restored Shakespeare's play in 1741 at the Theatre Royal, Drury Lane, reinstating the Gobbos, Morocco, and Aragon, but brought a passionate intensity to the role of Shylock that did much to establish the play as the moneylender's. Tubal also was returned, to heighten the effect of Shylock's scenes of outrage. A contemporary viewer reported that Shylock's calamities made "some tender impression on the audience," even though Shylock was at other times malevolent, cunning, and ferocious. He was, in other words, a complex figure, no longer a low comedy part as in Doggett's interpretation. Later eighteenth-century productions persisted in supplying various distractions—Morocco and Aragon were once again cut from the play, songs were supplied for Portia, Jessica, and Lorenzo by Thomas Arne and others, the casket scene was curtailed, and Kitty Clive amused audiences in her role of Portia by copying the mannerisms of certain well-known lawyers of the day—but the part of Shylock, even if not always conceived in a tragic vein, had proved a triumph for Macklin and was soon coveted by the leading actors of the eighteenth and nineteenth centuries.

George Frederick Cooke played Shylock in London first in 1800 and then, memorably, in 1803–1804, supported by John Philip Kemble, as Antonio, and Sarah Siddons, as Portia. Cooke's Shylock was, according to critic William Hazlitt, "bent with age and ugly with mental deformity, grinning with deadly malice, with the venom of his heart congealed in the expression of his countenance, sullen, morose, gloomy, inflexible." One version of the play, often performed during these years, featured an ending written by the Reverend Richard Valpy, with no fifth act at all but instead a recognition scene between Portia and Bassanio at the end of the trial; the play thus ended with the departure of its central figure, Shylock. Edmund Kean, at Drury Lane in 1814, the first actor to wear a black wig instead of the red wig of the stereotypical stage Jew, depicted Shylock with such scorn and energy that, to William Hazlitt at least, the Christians in the play were made to appear hypocrites by comparison. Romantic sympathies were turning in this direction, in any case; the older comedy of revenge and savagery seemed out of keeping with the play's love comedy and talk of mercy.

Victorian audiences were stirred not only by a sympathetic Shylock but by handsome sets calculated to enhance a mood of poetry, music, and romance. In 1841 at Drury Lane, William Charles Macready provided onstage a number of realistic scenes from Venice, including the cathedral and square of St. Mark's, Shylock's house facing on a canal with a distant view of the campanile, a court of justice reminiscent of the Roman Senate (as it had appeared before in Macready's revival of *Coriolanus*), and, most impressive of all, a moonlit garden in Act 5 that sparkled with soft light and melted away into poetic indistinctness toward the back of the set. Contemporary paintings of Act 5, such as those in John Boydell's Shakespeare gallery of art in Pall Mall, convey the kind of magical effect aimed at by Macready. At the Princess's Theatre in 1858 Charles Kean also began his production in St. Mark's Square, with milling crowds of noblemen and citizens, foreign visitors and flower girls, and the Doge in procession, all before the dialogue had begun. Edwin Booth's production of the play at the Winter Garden Theatre in New York in 1867 had magnificent scenery copied by Henry Hilliard and Charles Witham from famous paintings of well-known Venetian locales. In 1875 Sir Squire and Lady Bancroft, after a trip to Venice with their scene painter to select the sets, produced *The Merchant of Venice* at the Prince of Wales Theatre in Tottenham Court Road; because they could allow only one set to each act in their small theater, the play had to be rearranged considerably. The first tableau was located "under the arches of the Doge's palace," with a lovely view of the Church of Santa Maria della Salute. Merchants, sailors, beggars, and Jews passed and repassed in pantomimic action.

Henry Irving's lavish production at the Lyceum Theatre, London, in 1879 was thus only one, though perhaps the most famous, among a series of splendid visual evocations of Venice and Belmont. Continuing the tradition, begun by Charles Kean, of a usable bridge over the canals in the stage set, Irving employed this location for a memorable staging effect. He placed the elopement of Jessica in a season of carnival celebration: masked crowds walked about, gondolas arrived at waterside, merrymakers raced across the bridge. Shylock's return across the bridge alone to his dark and deserted house introduced a moment of supreme pathos that audiences, and a number of subsequent Shylocks, were quite unable to resist. At the trial scene a crowd of Jews followed the fate of Shylock with avid interest, listening intently to Portia's legal arguments and despairing of the outcome. Irving played Shylock as an aristocrat of his ancient religion, looking down with calm pride on the Europeans and then lashing out in rage and scorn. The nobility added to the pathos. Herbert Beerbohm Tree, in 1908, continued the tradition, and there have been numerous sympathetic Shylocks since.

More recent productions have tended to use sympathy for Shylock as a way of emphasizing the problematic morality of the entire play. George C. Scott, in Joseph Papp's production for the New York Shakespeare Festival in 1962, portrayed Shylock as neither a villain nor a victim but as a desperately defensive, paranoid, and persecuted man. In England, Laurence Olivier, in Jonathan Miller's National Theatre production of 1970 (subsequently televised), expressed through Shylock's long cry of pain as he left the courtroom the anguish of a bereaved and wronged man. The production, set in nineteenth-century Venice, took an unromantic look at the hypocrisy of the Christian community in that city, at its closed and bigoted world of privilege, at its complacent and mercantile ways. The playing of Jewish sacred music during the final scene reminded audiences that the feast of reconciliation at Belmont was achieved by excluding those who did not "belong."

A production at Stratford-upon-Avon in 1953 emphasized the friendship of Antonio and Bassanio in contrast to the solitariness of Michael Redgrave's wily and heavily accented Shylock, and other productions, such as Michael Kahn's at Stratford, Connecticut, in 1967, have gone so far as to see a homoerotic attraction between the Christian friends of this play.

Portia, in modern times, not infrequently becomes something of a calculating vixen, catty in her evaluation of her masculine wooers, insincere in her profession of hospitality to Morocco, ready to cheat by giving unfair hints to Bassanio in the casket scene (as in Theodore Komisarjevsky's production at Stratford-upon-Avon in 1932, in which Portia, singing "Tell me where is fancy bred," heavily stressed the words rhyming with "lead"), and adept at tormenting him in the episode of the rings. Jessica and Lorenzo can be portrayed as thoughtless in their frivolous dissipating of Shylock's wealth and keepsakes. As productions have returned to a full text, the earlier dominance of Shylock has made way for a ceaseless exploration of the play's provocative ambivalence, as, for example, in John Barton's 1978 production at London's Other Place, which sought to make both Shylock and the mercantile world of the Christians psychologically credible. The Merchant of Venice has increasingly been seen as one of Shakespeare's problem plays.

Shakespeare's original production had no scenery and so had to rely on costumed actors and on Shakespeare's language to conjure up a sense of place. The contrasts and similarities between Venice and Belmont built into the text must have called for an alternating rhythm of staging effects in the movement back and forth from largely male scenes of business and legal disputation in Venice to scenes of feminine wit, badinage, and the unveiling of caskets in Belmont. Shylock's house was visually invoked in the Elizabethan theater by Jessica's appearance "above" in the gallery, as at Shylock's window; from this vantage she could throw down money to the maskers below in the street before exiting above and then joining them on the main stage for the elopement (2.6). The trial scene (4.1) was visualized presumably by means of robed justices in their seats, by Portia in disguise as a doctor of laws, by Shylock with his bond and his knife, and by an atmosphere of confrontation. The actors established the mood of Belmont in Act 5 chiefly by their talk about the starry night and by their recollection of old tales about the tribulations of love. Twentieth-century theater has attempted, by and large, to find new theatrical ways of suggesting these effects in place of the heavy representational sets of the nineteenth century, recognizing that theater should not mechanically replicate what Shakespeare calls for in the image-laden language of his characters. Above all, staging today seems intent on capturing the dark ambivalences that are so integrally a part of the play's stage history.

The Playhouse

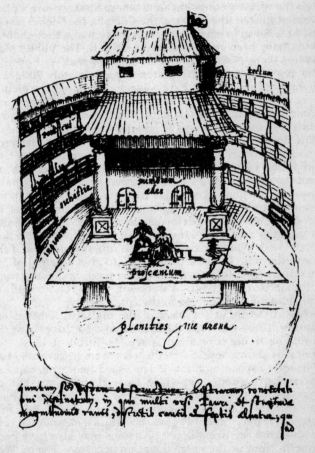

This early copy of a drawing by Johannes de Witt of the Swan Theatre in London (c. 1596), made by his friend Arend van Buchell, is the only surviving contemporary sketch of the interior of a public theater in the 1590s.

From other contemporary evidence, including the stage directions and dialogue of Elizabethan plays, we can surmise that the various public theaters where Shakespeare's plays were produced (the Theatre, the Curtain, the Globe) resembled the Swan in many important particulars, though there must have been some variations as well. The public playhouses were essentially round, or polygonal, and open to the sky, forming an acting arena approximately 70 feet in diameter; they did not have a large curtain with which to open and close a scene, such as we see today in opera and some traditional theater. A platform measuring approximately 43 feet across and 27 feet deep, referred to in the de Witt drawing as the *proscaenium*, projected into the yard, *planities sive arena*. The roof, *tectum*, above the stage and supported by two pillars, could contain machinery for ascents and descents, as were required in several of Shakespeare's late plays. Above this roof was a hut, shown in the drawing with a flag flying atop it and a trumpeter at its door announcing the performance of a play. The underside of the stage roof, called the heavens, was usually richly decorated with symbolic figures of the sun, the moon, and the constellations. The platform stage stood at a height of 5½ feet or so above the yard, providing room under the stage for underworldly effects. A trapdoor, which is not visible in this drawing, gave access to the space below.

The structure at the back of the platform (labeled *mimorum aedes*), known as the tiring-house because it was the actors' attiring (dressing) space, featured at least two doors, as shown here. Some theaters seem to have also had a discovery space, or curtained recessed alcove, perhaps between the two doors—in which Falstaff could have hidden from the sheriff (*1 Henry IV*, 2.4) or Polonius could have eavesdropped on Hamlet and his mother (*Hamlet*, 3.4). This discovery space probably gave the actors a means of access to and from the tiring-house. Curtains may also have been hung in front of the stage doors on occasion. The de Witt drawing shows a gallery above the doors that extends across the back and evidently contains spectators. On occasions when action "above" demanded the use of this space, as when Juliet appears at her "window" (*Romeo and Juliet*, 2.2 and 3.5), the gallery seems to have been used by the actors, but large scenes there were impractical.

The three-tiered auditorium is perhaps best described by Thomas Platter, a visitor to London in 1599 who saw on that occasion Shakespeare's *Julius Caesar* performed at the Globe:

> The playhouses are so constructed that they play on a raised platform, so that everyone has a good view. There are different galleries and places [*orchestra, sedilia, porticus*], however, where the seating is better and more comfortable and therefore more expensive. For whoever cares to stand below only pays one English penny, but if he wishes to sit, he enters by another door [*ingressus*] and pays another penny, while if he desires to sit in the most comfortable seats, which are cushioned, where he not only sees everything well but can also be seen, then he pays yet another English penny at another door. And during the performance food and drink are carried round the audience, so that for what one cares to pay one may also have refreshment.

Scenery was not used, though the theater building itself was handsome enough to invoke a feeling of order and hierarchy that lent itself to the splendor and pageantry onstage. Portable properties, such as thrones, stools, tables, and beds, could be carried or thrust on as needed. In the scene pictured here by de Witt, a lady on a bench, attended perhaps by her waiting-gentlewoman, receives the address of a male figure. If Shakespeare had written *Twelfth Night* by 1596 for performance at the Swan, we could imagine Malvolio appearing like this as he bows before the Countess Olivia and her gentlewoman, Maria.

THE MERCHANT
OF VENICE

1.1   *Enter Antonio, Salerio, and Solanio.*

ANTONIO
In sooth, I know not why I am so sad.
It wearies me, you say it wearies you;
But how I caught it, found it, or came by it,
What stuff 'tis made of, whereof it is born,
I am to learn;   5
And such a want-wit sadness makes of me   6
That I have much ado to know myself.
SALERIO
Your mind is tossing on the ocean,
There where your argosies with portly sail,   9
Like signors and rich burghers on the flood,   10
Or as it were the pageants of the sea,   11
Do overpeer the petty traffickers   12
That curtsy to them, do them reverence   13
As they fly by them with their woven wings.
SOLANIO
Believe me, sir, had I such venture forth,   15
The better part of my affections would
Be with my hopes abroad. I should be still   17
Plucking the grass to know where sits the wind,
Peering in maps for ports and piers and roads;   19
And every object that might make me fear
Misfortune to my ventures, out of doubt
Would make me sad.
SALERIO   My wind cooling my broth
Would blow me to an ague when I thought
What harm a wind too great might do at sea.
I should not see the sandy hourglass run
But I should think of shallows and of flats,   26
And see my wealthy *Andrew* docked in sand,   27

1.1. Location: A street in Venice.
5 am to learn have yet to learn   **6 want-wit** one lacking in good sense
9 argosies large merchant ships. (So named from *Ragusa,* the modern
city of Dubrovnik.)   **portly** majestic   **10 signors** gentlemen
11 pageants mobile stages used in plays or processions   **12 overpeer**
look down upon   **13 curtsy** i.e., bob up and down   **15 venture forth**
investment risked   **17 still** continually   **19 roads** anchorages, open
harbors   **26 But** without it happening that.   **flats** shoals   **27 Andrew**
name of a ship (perhaps after the *St. Andrew,* a Spanish galleon captured at Cadiz in 1596)

Vailing her high-top lower than her ribs   28
To kiss her burial. Should I go to church   29
And see the holy edifice of stone,
And not bethink me straight of dangerous rocks,   31
Which touching but my gentle vessel's side
Would scatter all her spices on the stream,
Enrobe the roaring waters with my silks,
And, in a word, but even now worth this,   35
And now worth nothing? Shall I have the thought
To think on this, and shall I lack the thought
That such a thing bechanced would make me sad?   38
But tell not me; I know Antonio
Is sad to think upon his merchandise.

ANTONIO
Believe me, no. I thank my fortune for it,
My ventures are not in one bottom trusted,   42
Nor to one place; nor is my whole estate
Upon the fortune of this present year.   44
Therefore my merchandise makes me not sad.

SOLANIO
Why, then you are in love.

ANTONIO   Fie, fie!

SOLANIO
Not in love neither? Then let us say you are sad
Because you are not merry; and 'twere as easy
For you to laugh and leap, and say you are merry
Because you are not sad. Now, by two-headed Janus,   50
Nature hath framed strange fellows in her time:
Some that will evermore peep through their eyes
And laugh like parrots at a bagpiper,   53
And other of such vinegar aspect   54
That they'll not show their teeth in way of smile
Though Nestor swear the jest be laughable.   56

28 Vailing lowering (usually as a sign of submission). **high-top** top-
mast **29 burial** burial place **31 bethink me straight** be put in mind
immediately **35 this** i.e., all this concern **38 bechanced** having happened **42 bottom** ship's hold **44 Upon . . . year** i.e., risked upon the
chance of the present **50 two-headed Janus** a Roman god of all begin-
nings, represented by a figure with two faces **53 at a bagpiper** i.e.,
even at a bagpiper, whose music was regarded as melancholic
54 vinegar sour, sullen **56 Nestor** venerable senior officer in the *Iliad*,
noted for gravity

Enter Bassanio, Lorenzo, and Gratiano.

Here comes Bassanio, your most noble kinsman,
Gratiano, and Lorenzo. Fare ye well.
We leave you now with better company.

SALERIO
I would have stayed till I had made you merry,
If worthier friends had not prevented me.   61

ANTONIO
Your worth is very dear in my regard.
I take it your own business calls on you,
And you embrace th' occasion to depart.   64

SALERIO   Good morrow, my good lords.

BASSANIO
Good signors both, when shall we laugh? Say, when?   66
You grow exceeding strange. Must it be so?   67

SALERIO
We'll make our leisures to attend on yours.   68
                          Exeunt Salerio and Solanio.

LORENZO
My lord Bassanio, since you have found Antonio,
We two will leave you, but at dinnertime,
I pray you, have in mind where we must meet.

BASSANIO   I will not fail you.

GRATIANO
You look not well, Signor Antonio.
You have too much respect upon the world;   74
They lose it that do buy it with much care.
Believe me, you are marvelously changed.

ANTONIO
I hold the world but as the world, Gratiano,
A stage where every man must play a part,
And mine a sad one.

GRATIANO   Let me play the fool!
With mirth and laughter let old wrinkles come,
And let my liver rather heat with wine   81

61 prevented forestalled **64 occasion** opportunity **66 laugh** i.e., be
merry together **67 strange** distant. **Must it be so** must you go; or,
must you show reserve **68 attend on** wait upon, i.e., suit **74 respect
. . . world** concern for worldly affairs of business **81 heat with wine**
(The liver was regarded as the seat of the passions and wine as an
agency for inflaming them.)

Than my heart cool with mortifying groans.   82
Why should a man whose blood is warm within
Sit like his grandsire cut in alabaster?   84
Sleep when he wakes, and creep into the jaundice   85
By being peevish? I tell thee what, Antonio—
I love thee, and 'tis my love that speaks—
There are a sort of men whose visages
Do cream and mantle like a standing pond,   89
And do a willful stillness entertain   90
With purpose to be dressed in an opinion   91
Of wisdom, gravity, profound conceit,   92
As who should say, "I am Sir Oracle,   93
And when I ope my lips let no dog bark!"   94
O my Antonio, I do know of these
That therefore only are reputed wise
For saying nothing, when, I am very sure,
If they should speak, would almost damn those ears
Which, hearing them, would call their brothers fools.   99
I'll tell thee more of this another time.
But fish not with this melancholy bait   101
For this fool gudgeon, this opinion.   102
Come, good Lorenzo. Fare ye well awhile;
I'll end my exhortation after dinner.

LORENZO
Well, we will leave you then till dinnertime.
I must be one of these same dumb wise men,   106
For Gratiano never lets me speak.

GRATIANO
Well, keep me company but two years more,
Thou shalt not know the sound of thine own tongue.

---

82 mortifying deadly   **84 in alabaster** i.e., in a stone effigy upon a
tomb   **85 jaundice** (Regarded as arising from the effects of too much
choler or yellow bile, one of the four humors, in the blood.)   **89 cream
and mantle** become covered with scum, i.e., acquire a lifeless, stiff
expression.   **90 And . . . entertain** and who maintain
or assume a self-imposed, obstinate silence   **91 opinion** reputation
92 profound conceit deep thought   **93 As . . . say** as if to say   **94 And
. . . bark** i.e., and I am worthy of great respect   **99 fools** (Cf. Matthew
5:22, in which anyone calling another fool is threatened with damnation.)   **101 melancholy bait** i.e., your own melancholy   **102 fool . . .
opinion** i.e., reputation, which is merely gained through others' credu-
lity. (*Gudgeon*, a small fish, was used to mean a gullible person.)
106 dumb mute, speechless

ANTONIO
  Fare you well; I'll grow a talker for this gear.   110
GRATIANO
  Thanks, i' faith, for silence is only commendable
  In a neat's tongue dried and a maid not vendible.   112
                    Exeunt [Gratiano and Lorenzo].
ANTONIO   Is that anything now?   113
BASSANIO   Gratiano speaks an infinite deal of nothing,
  more than any man in all Venice. His reasons are as
  two grains of wheat hid in two bushels of chaff; you
  shall seek all day ere you find them, and when you
  have them they are not worth the search.
ANTONIO
  Well, tell me now what lady is the same   119
  To whom you swore a secret pilgrimage,
  That you today promised to tell me of.
BASSANIO
  'Tis not unknown to you, Antonio,
  How much I have disabled mine estate
  By something showing a more swelling port   124
  Than my faint means would grant continuance.   125
  Nor do I now make moan to be abridged   126
  From such a noble rate; but my chief care   127
  Is to come fairly off from the great debts   128
  Wherein my time, something too prodigal,
  Hath left me gaged. To you, Antonio,   130
  I owe the most, in money and in love,
  And from your love I have a warranty   132
  To unburden all my plots and purposes
  How to get clear of all the debts I owe.
ANTONIO
  I pray you, good Bassanio, let me know it;
  And if it stand, as you yourself still do,
  Within the eye of honor, be assured

110 for this gear as a result of this business, i.e., your talk   **112 neat's**
ox's.   **vendible** salable, i.e., in the marriage market   **113 Is . . . now** i.e.,
was all that talk about anything?   **119 the same** i.e., the one   **124 By
. . . port** by showing a somewhat more lavish style of living   **125 grant
continuance** allow to continue   **126–127 make . . . rate** complain at
being cut back from such a high style of living   **128 to . . . off** honor-
ably to extricate myself   **130 gaged** pledged   **132 warranty** authorization

My purse, my person, my extremest means,
Lie all unlocked to your occasions.

BASSANIO

In my schooldays, when I had lost one shaft,   140
I shot his fellow of the selfsame flight   141
The selfsame way with more advisèd watch   142
To find the other forth, and by adventuring both   143
I oft found both. I urge this childhood proof
Because what follows is pure innocence.   145
I owe you much, and, like a willful youth,
That which I owe is lost; but if you please
To shoot another arrow that self way   148
Which you did shoot the first, I do not doubt,
As I will watch the aim, or to find both   150
Or bring your latter hazard back again   151
And thankfully rest debtor for the first.

ANTONIO

You know me well, and herein spend but time   153
To wind about my love with circumstance;   154
And out of doubt you do me now more wrong   155
In making question of my uttermost   156
Than if you had made waste of all I have.
Then do but say to me what I should do
That in your knowledge may by me be done,
And I am prest unto it. Therefore speak.   160

BASSANIO

In Belmont is a lady richly left;   161
And she is fair and, fairer than that word,
Of wondrous virtues. Sometime from her eyes   163
I did receive fair speechless messages.
Her name is Portia, nothing undervalued   165
To Cato's daughter, Brutus' Portia.   166

---

140 shaft arrow   **141 his** its.   **selfsame flight** same kind and range
142 advisèd careful   **143 forth** out.   **adventuring** risking   **145 innocence** ingenuousness, sincerity   **148 self** same   **150 or** either   **151 hazard** that which was risked   **153 spend but time** only waste time   **154 To
. . . circumstance** i.e., in not asking plainly what you want. (*Circumstance* here means "circumlocution.")   **155 out of** beyond   **156 In . . .
uttermost** in showing any doubt of my intention to do all I can
160 prest ready   **161 richly left** left a large fortune (by her father's
will)   **163 Sometime** once   **165–166 nothing undervalued To** of no less
worth than   **166 Portia** (The same Portia as in Shakespeare's *Julius
Caesar*.)

Nor is the wide world ignorant of her worth,
For the four winds blow in from every coast
Renownèd suitors, and her sunny locks
Hang on her temples like a golden fleece,
Which makes her seat of Belmont Colchis' strand,   171
And many Jasons come in quest of her.
O my Antonio, had I but the means
To hold a rival place with one of them,
I have a mind presages me such thrift   175
That I should questionless be fortunate.

ANTONIO
Thou know'st that all my fortunes are at sea;
Neither have I money nor commodity   178
To raise a present sum. Therefore go forth.
Try what my credit can in Venice do;
That shall be racked, even to the uttermost,   181
To furnish thee to Belmont, to fair Portia.
Go presently inquire, and so will I,   183
Where money is, and I no question make   184
To have it of my trust or for my sake.   *Exeunt.*   185

❖

1.2   *Enter Portia with her waiting-woman, Nerissa.*

PORTIA   By my troth, Nerissa, my little body is aweary
of this great world.
NERISSA   You would be, sweet madam, if your miseries
were in the same abundance as your good fortunes
are; and yet, for aught I see, they are as sick that surfeit 5
with too much as they that starve with nothing. It is
no mean happiness, therefore, to be seated in the 7
mean; superfluity comes sooner by white hairs, but 8
competency lives longer. 9

171 Colchis' (Jason adventured for the golden fleece in the land of
Colchis, on the Black Sea.)   **strand** shore   **175 presages** i.e., which
presages.   **thrift** profit and good fortune   **178 commodity** merchandise   **181 racked** stretched   **183 presently** immediately   **184 no question make** have no doubt   **185 of my trust** on the basis of my credit as
a merchant.   **sake** i.e., personal sake

1.2. Location: Belmont. Portia's house.
5 surfeit overindulge   **7–8 in the mean** having neither too much nor too
little   **8 comes sooner by** acquires sooner   **9 competency** modest means

PORTIA Good sentences, and well pronounced.   10
NERISSA They would be better if well followed.
PORTIA If to do were as easy as to know what were
good to do, chapels had been churches and poor
men's cottages princes' palaces. It is a good divine that 14
follows his own instructions. I can easier teach twenty
what were good to be done than to be one of the
twenty to follow mine own teaching. The brain may
devise laws for the blood, but a hot temper leaps o'er 18
a cold decree—such a hare is madness the youth, to
skip o'er the meshes of good counsel the cripple. But 20
this reasoning is not in the fashion to choose me a 21
husband. O, me, the word "choose"! I may neither 22
choose who I would nor refuse who I dislike; so is the
will of a living daughter curbed by the will of a dead 24
father. Is it not hard, Nerissa, that I cannot choose one
nor refuse none?
NERISSA Your father was ever virtuous, and holy men
at their death have good inspirations; therefore the
lottery that he hath devised in these three chests of
gold, silver, and lead, whereof who chooses his mean- 30
ing chooses you, will no doubt never be chosen by
any rightly but one who you shall rightly love. But
what warmth is there in your affection towards any of
these princely suitors that are already come?
PORTIA I pray thee, overname them, and as thou nam- 35
est them I will describe them, and according to my
description level at my affection.   37
NERISSA First, there is the Neapolitan prince.
PORTIA Ay, that's a colt indeed, for he doth nothing but 39
talk of his horse, and he makes it a great appropriation 40
to his own good parts that he can shoe him him- 41

---

10 sentences maxims. **pronounced** delivered   **14 divine** clergyman
18 blood (Thought of as a chief agent of the passions, which in turn
were regarded as the enemies of reason.)   **20 meshes** nets (used here for
hunting hares).   **good counsel the cripple** (Wisdom is portrayed as old
and no longer agile.)   **20–22 But . . . husband** but this talk is not the
way to help me choose a husband   **24 will . . . will** volition . . . testament   **30 who** whoever.   **his** i.e., the father's   **35 overname them** name
them over   **37 level** aim, guess   **39 colt** i.e., wanton and foolish young
man (with a punning appropriateness to his interest in horses)
40 appropriation addition   **41 good parts** accomplishments

self. I am much afeard my lady his mother played false
with a smith.

NERISSA   Then is there the County Palatine.   44

PORTIA   He doth nothing but frown, as who should say,   45
"An you will not have me, choose." He hears merry   46
tales and smiles not. I fear he will prove the weeping   47
philosopher when he grows old, being so full of un-   48
mannerly sadness in his youth. I had rather be married to a death's-head with a bone in his mouth than
to either of these. God defend me from these two!

NERISSA   How say you by the French lord, Monsieur   52
Le Bon?

PORTIA   God made him, and therefore let him pass for
a man. In truth, I know it is a sin to be a mocker, but
he! Why, he hath a horse better than the Neapolitan's,
a better bad habit of frowning than the Count Palatine; he is every man in no man. If a throstle sing, he   58
falls straight a-capering. He will fence with his own
shadow. If I should marry him, I should marry twenty
husbands. If he would despise me, I would forgive
him, for if he love me to madness, I shall never requite him.

NERISSA   What say you, then, to Falconbridge, the
young baron of England?

PORTIA   You know I say nothing to him, for he under-
stands not me, nor I him. He hath neither Latin,
French, nor Italian, and you will come into the court
and swear that I have a poor pennyworth in the English. He is a proper man's picture, but alas, who can   70
converse with a dumb show? How oddly he is suited!   71
I think he bought his doublet in Italy, his round hose   72
in France, his bonnet in Germany, and his behavior   73
everywhere.

---

44 County count. **Palatine** one possessing royal privileges   **45 who
should say** one might say   **46 An** if. **choose** i.e., do as you please
47–48 weeping philosopher i.e., Heraclitus of Ephesus, a melancholic
and retiring philosopher of about 500 B.C., often contrasted with Demo-
critus, the "laughing philosopher"   **52 by** about   **58 throstle** thrush
70 He . . . picture i.e., he looks handsome   **71 dumb show** panto-
mime. **suited** dressed   **72 doublet** upper garment corresponding to a
jacket. **round hose** short, puffed-out breeches   **73 bonnet** hat

NERISSA What think you of the Scottish lord, his
neighbor?

PORTIA That he hath a neighborly charity in him, for he
borrowed a box of the ear of the Englishman and swore
he would pay him again when he was able. I think the
Frenchman became his surety and sealed under for an- 80
other.   81

NERISSA How like you the young German, the Duke of
Saxony's nephew?

PORTIA Very vilely in the morning, when he is sober,
and most vilely in the afternoon, when he is drunk.
When he is best he is a little worse than a man, and
when he is worst he is little better than a beast. An
the worst fall that ever fell, I hope I shall make shift to 88
go without him.

NERISSA If he should offer to choose, and choose the
right casket, you should refuse to perform your father's
will if you should refuse to accept him.

PORTIA Therefore, for fear of the worst, I pray thee, set
a deep glass of Rhenish wine on the contrary casket, 94
for if the devil be within and that temptation without,
I know he will choose it. I will do anything, Nerissa,
ere I will be married to a sponge.

NERISSA You need not fear, lady, the having any of
these lords. They have acquainted me with their de-
terminations, which is indeed to return to their home
and to trouble you with no more suit, unless you may
be won by some other sort than your father's imposi- 102
tion depending on the caskets.   103

PORTIA If I live to be as old as Sibylla, I will die as chaste 104
as Diana, unless I be obtained by the manner of my
father's will. I am glad this parcel of wooers are so rea- 106
sonable, for there is not one among them but I dote on

80–81 became . . . another guaranteed the Scot's payment (of a box on
the ear) and put himself under obligation to give the Englishman yet
another on his own behalf. (An allusion to the age-old alliance of the
French and the Scots against the English.) **88 fall** befall. **make shift**
manage **94 Rhenish wine** a German white wine from the Rhine Valley. **contrary** i.e., wrong **102 sort** way, manner (with perhaps a suggestion too of "casting" or "drawing of lots") **102–103 imposition**
conditions imposed **104 Sibylla** the Cumaean Sibyl, to whom Apollo
gave as many years as there were grains in her handful of sand
106 parcel assembly, group

his very absence, and I pray God grant them a fair
departure.

NERISSA Do you not remember, lady, in your father's
time, a Venetian, a scholar and a soldier, that came
hither in company of the Marquess of Montferrat?

PORTIA Yes, yes, it was Bassanio, as I think, so was he
called.

NERISSA True, madam. He, of all the men that ever my
foolish eyes looked upon, was the best deserving a fair
lady.

PORTIA I remember him well, and I remember him
worthy of thy praise.

    Enter a Servingman.

How now, what news?

SERVINGMAN The four strangers seek for you, madam,   121
to take their leave; and there is a forerunner come from   122
a fifth, the Prince of Morocco, who brings word the
Prince his master will be here tonight.

PORTIA If I could bid the fifth welcome with so good
heart as I can bid the other four farewell, I should be
glad of his approach. If he have the condition of a saint   127
and the complexion of a devil, I had rather he should   128
shrive me than wive me.   129
Come, Nerissa. [*To Servingman.*] Sirrah, go before.   130
Whiles we shut the gate upon one wooer, another
   knocks at the door.   *Exeunt.*

❖

1.3 *Enter Bassanio with Shylock the Jew.*

SHYLOCK Three thousand ducats, well.   1
BASSANIO Ay, sir, for three months.
SHYLOCK For three months, well.

121 four (Nerissa actually names six suitors; possibly a sign of revi-
sion.) **122 forerunner** herald **127 condition** disposition, character
128 complexion of a devil (Devils were thought to be black; but *complexion* can also mean "temperament," "disposition.") **129 shrive
me** act as my confessor **130 Sirrah** (Form of address to social infe-
rior.)

1.3. Location: Venice. A public place.
1 ducats gold coins

BASSANIO   For the which, as I told you, Antonio shall be
bound.

SHYLOCK   Antonio shall become bound, well.

BASSANIO   May you stead me? Will you pleasure me? 7
Shall I know your answer?

SHYLOCK   Three thousand ducats for three months and
Antonio bound.

BASSANIO   Your answer to that.

SHYLOCK   Antonio is a good man.   12

BASSANIO   Have you heard any imputation to the contrary?

SHYLOCK   Ho, no, no, no, no! My meaning in saying he
is a good man is to have you understand me that he is
sufficient. Yet his means are in supposition: he hath an 17
argosy bound to Tripolis, another to the Indies; I understand, moreover, upon the Rialto, he hath a 19
third at Mexico, a fourth for England, and other ventures he hath squandered abroad. But ships are but 21
boards, sailors but men; there be land rats and water
rats, water thieves and land thieves—I mean pirates—
and then there is the peril of waters, winds, and rocks.
The man is, notwithstanding, sufficient. Three thousand ducats; I think I may take his bond.

BASSANIO   Be assured you may.   27

SHYLOCK   I will be assured I may; and that I may be 28
assured, I will bethink me. May I speak with Antonio?

BASSANIO   If it please you to dine with us.

SHYLOCK   Yes, to smell pork, to eat of the habitation
which your prophet the Nazarite conjured the devil 32
into. I will buy with you, sell with you, talk with you,
walk with you, and so following, but I will not eat
with you, drink with you, nor pray with you. What
news on the Rialto? Who is he comes here?

---

7 stead supply, assist   **12 good** (Shylock means "solvent," a good credit
risk; Bassanio interprets in the moral sense.)   **17 sufficient** i.e., a good
security.   **in supposition** doubtful, uncertain   **19 Rialto** the merchants'
exchange in Venice and the center of commercial activity   **21 squandered** scattered, spread   **27, 28 assured** (Bassanio means that
Shylock may trust Antonio, whereas Shylock means that he will provide
legal assurances.)   **32 Nazarite** Nazarene. (For the reference to Christ's
casting evil spirits into a herd of swine, see Matthew 8:30–32, Mark
5:1–13, and Luke 8:32–33.)

Enter Antonio.

BASSANIO   This is Signor Antonio.

SHYLOCK *[Aside]*

How like a fawning publican he looks!   38
I hate him for he is a Christian,   39
But more for that in low simplicity
He lends out money gratis and brings down
The rate of usance here with us in Venice.   42
If I can catch him once upon the hip,   43
I will feed fat the ancient grudge I bear him.
He hates our sacred nation, and he rails,
Even there where merchants most do congregate,
On me, my bargains, and my well-won thrift,   47
Which he calls interest. Cursèd be my tribe
If I forgive him!

BASSANIO   Shylock, do you hear?

SHYLOCK

I am debating of my present store,   50
And, by the near guess of my memory,
I cannot instantly raise up the gross   52
Of full three thousand ducats. What of that?
Tubal, a wealthy Hebrew of my tribe,
Will furnish me. But soft, how many months   55
Do you desire? *[To Antonio.]* Rest you fair, good signor!
Your worship was the last man in our mouths.   57

ANTONIO

Shylock, albeit I neither lend nor borrow
By taking nor by giving of excess,   59
Yet, to supply the ripe wants of my friend,   60
I'll break a custom. *[To Bassanio.]* Is he yet possessed   61
How much ye would?

SHYLOCK   Ay, ay, three thousand ducats.

ANTONIO   And for three months.

SHYLOCK

I had forgot—three months, you told me so.

---

38 publican Roman tax gatherer (a term of opprobrium); or, innkeeper
39 for because   **42 usance** usury, interest   **43 upon the hip** i.e., at my
mercy. (A figure of speech from wrestling; see Genesis 32:24–29.)
47 thrift thriving   **50 store** supply (of money)   **52 gross** total   **55 soft**
i.e., wait a minute   **57 Your . . . mouths** i.e., we were just speaking of
you   **59 excess** interest   **60 ripe wants** pressing needs   **61 possessed**
informed

Well then, your bond. And let me see—but hear you,
Methought you said you neither lend nor borrow
Upon advantage.

ANTONIO   I do never use it.   68

SHYLOCK
When Jacob grazed his uncle Laban's sheep—   69
This Jacob from our holy Abram was,   70
As his wise mother wrought in his behalf,
The third possessor; ay, he was the third—   72

ANTONIO
And what of him? Did he take interest?

SHYLOCK
No, not take interest, not as you would say
Directly interest. Mark what Jacob did.
When Laban and himself were compromised   76
That all the eanlings which were streaked and pied   77
Should fall as Jacob's hire, the ewes, being rank,   78
In end of autumn turnèd to the rams,
And when the work of generation was
Between these woolly breeders in the act,
The skillful shepherd peeled me certain wands,   82
And in the doing of the deed of kind   83
He stuck them up before the fulsome ewes,
Who then conceiving did in eaning time   85
Fall parti-colored lambs, and those were Jacob's.   86
This was a way to thrive, and he was blest;
And thrift is blessing, if men steal it not.

ANTONIO
This was a venture, sir, that Jacob served for,   89
A thing not in his power to bring to pass,
But swayed and fashioned by the hand of heaven.
Was this inserted to make interest good?   92
Or is your gold and silver ewes and rams?

---

68 advantage interest   **69 Jacob** (See Genesis 27, 30:25–43.)   **70 Abram**
Abraham   **72 third** i.e., after Abraham and Isaac.   **possessor** i.e., of the
birthright of which, with the help of Rebecca, he was able to cheat
Esau, his elder brother   **76 compromised** agreed   **77 eanlings** young
lambs or kids.   **pied** spotted   **78 hire** wages, share.   **rank** in heat
82 me (*Me* is used colloquially.)   **83 deed of kind** i.e., copulation
85 eaning lambing   **86 Fall** give birth to   **89 venture . . . for** uncertain
commercial venture on which Jacob risked his wages   **92 inserted . . .
good** brought in to justify the practice of usury

SHYLOCK
  I cannot tell; I make it breed as fast.
  But note me, signor—
ANTONIO   Mark you this, Bassanio,
  The devil can cite Scripture for his purpose.   96
  An evil soul producing holy witness
  Is like a villain with a smiling cheek,
  A goodly apple rotten at the heart.
  O, what a goodly outside falsehood hath!
SHYLOCK
  Three thousand ducats. 'Tis a good round sum.
  Three months from twelve, then let me see, the rate—
ANTONIO
  Well, Shylock, shall we be beholding to you?   103
SHYLOCK
  Signor Antonio, many a time and oft
  In the Rialto you have rated me   105
  About my moneys and my usances.
  Still have I borne it with a patient shrug,
  For sufferance is the badge of all our tribe.   108
  You call me misbeliever, cutthroat dog,
  And spit upon my Jewish gaberdine,   110
  And all for use of that which is mine own.
  Well then, it now appears you need my help.
  Go to, then. You come to me and you say,   113
  "Shylock, we would have moneys"—you say so,
  You, that did void your rheum upon my beard   115
  And foot me as you spurn a stranger cur   116
  Over your threshold! Moneys is your suit.
  What should I say to you? Should I not say,
  "Hath a dog money? Is it possible
  A cur can lend three thousand ducats?" Or
  Shall I bend low and in a bondman's key,   121
  With bated breath and whispering humbleness,   122
  Say this:
  "Fair sir, you spit on me on Wednesday last,
  You spurned me such a day, another time

96 devil . . . Scripture (See Matthew 4:6.) **103 beholding** beholden,
indebted **105 rated** berated, rebuked **108 sufferance** endurance
110 gaberdine loose upper garment like a cape or mantle **113 Go to**
(An exclamation of impatience or annoyance.) **115 rheum** spittle
116 spurn kick **121 bondman's** serf's **122 bated** subdued, reduced

You called me dog, and for these courtesies
I'll lend you thus much moneys"?

ANTONIO
I am as like to call thee so again,   128
To spit on thee again, to spurn thee too.
If thou wilt lend this money, lend it not
As to thy friends, for when did friendship take
A breed for barren metal of his friend?   132
But lend it rather to thine enemy,
Who, if he break, thou mayst with better face   134
Exact the penalty.

SHYLOCK   Why, look you how you storm!
I would be friends with you and have your love,
Forget the shames that you have stained me with,
Supply your present wants, and take no doit   138
Of usance for my moneys, and you'll not hear me.
This is kind I offer.

BASSANIO   This were kindness.   141

SHYLOCK   This kindness will I show.
Go with me to a notary. Seal me there
Your single bond; and, in a merry sport,   144
If you repay me not on such a day,
In such a place, such sum or sums as are
Expressed in the condition, let the forfeit
Be nominated for an equal pound   148
Of your fair flesh, to be cut off and taken
In what part of your body pleaseth me.

ANTONIO
Content, in faith. I'll seal to such a bond
And say there is much kindness in the Jew.

BASSANIO
You shall not seal to such a bond for me!
I'll rather dwell in my necessity.   154

ANTONIO
Why, fear not, man, I will not forfeit it.

---

128 like likely   **132 breed . . . metal** offspring from money, which
cannot naturally breed. (One of the oldest arguments against usury was
that it was thereby "unnatural.")   **134 Who** from whom.   **break** fail to
pay on time   **138 doit** a Dutch coin of very small value   **141 were**
would be (if seriously offered)   **144 single bond** bond signed alone
without other security   **148 nominated** named, specified.   **equal**
exact   **154 dwell** remain

Within these two months—that's a month before
This bond expires—I do expect return
Of thrice three times the value of this bond.

SHYLOCK
O father Abram, what these Christians are,
Whose own hard dealings teaches them suspect
The thoughts of others! Pray you, tell me this:
If he should break his day, what should I gain
By the exaction of the forfeiture?
A pound of man's flesh taken from a man
Is not so estimable, profitable neither,   165
As flesh of muttons, beefs, or goats. I say
To buy his favor I extend this friendship.
If he will take it, so; if not, adieu.
And for my love, I pray you, wrong me not.   169

ANTONIO
Yes, Shylock, I will seal unto this bond.

SHYLOCK
Then meet me forthwith at the notary's;
Give him direction for this merry bond,
And I will go and purse the ducats straight,
See to my house, left in the fearful guard   174
Of an unthrifty knave, and presently
I'll be with you.   *Exit.*

ANTONIO   Hie thee, gentle Jew.
The Hebrew will turn Christian; he grows kind.

BASSANIO
I like not fair terms and a villain's mind.

ANTONIO
Come on. In this there can be no dismay;
My ships come home a month before the day.

                                              Exeunt.

❖

165 estimable valuable   **169 wrong me not** do not think evil of me
174 fearful to be mistrusted

2.1 [*Flourish of cornets.*] *Enter* [*the Prince of*]
*Morocco, a tawny Moor all in white, and three
or four followers accordingly, with Portia,
Nerissa, and their train.*

MOROCCO
  Mislike me not for my complexion,
  The shadowed livery of the burnished sun,   2
  To whom I am a neighbor and near bred.   3
  Bring me the fairest creature northward born,
  Where Phoebus' fire scarce thaws the icicles,   5
  And let us make incision for your love
  To prove whose blood is reddest, his or mine.   7
  I tell thee, lady, this aspect of mine   8
  Hath feared the valiant. By my love I swear,   9
  The best-regarded virgins of our clime
  Have loved it too. I would not change this hue,
  Except to steal your thoughts, my gentle queen.
PORTIA
  In terms of choice I am not solely led
  By nice direction of a maiden's eyes;   14
  Besides, the lottery of my destiny
  Bars me the right of voluntary choosing.
  But if my father had not scanted me,   17
  And hedged me by his wit to yield myself   18
  His wife who wins me by that means I told you,
  Yourself, renownèd Prince, then stood as fair
  As any comer I have looked on yet
  For my affection.
MOROCCO   Even for that I thank you.
  Therefore, I pray you, lead me to the caskets
  To try my fortune. By this scimitar
  That slew the Sophy and a Persian prince,   25
  That won three fields of Sultan Solyman,   26

2.1. Location: Belmont. Portia's house.
s.d. accordingly similarly (i.e., dressed in white and dark-skinned like
Morocco) **2 shadowed livery** i.e., dark complexion, worn as though it
were a costume of the sun's servants **3 near bred** closely related
5 Phoebus' i.e., the sun's **7 reddest** (Red blood was regarded as a sign
of courage.) **8 aspect** visage **9 feared** frightened **14 nice direction**
careful guidance **17 scanted** limited **18 wit** wisdom **25 Sophy** Shah
of Persia **26 fields** battles. **Solyman** a Turkish sultan ruling 1520–1566

I would o'erstare the sternest eyes that look,   27
Outbrave the heart most daring on the earth,
Pluck the young sucking cubs from the she-bear,
Yea, mock the lion when 'a roars for prey,   30
To win thee, lady. But alas the while!
If Hercules and Lichas play at dice   32
Which is the better man, the greater throw
May turn by fortune from the weaker hand.
So is Alcides beaten by his page,
And so may I, blind Fortune leading me,
Miss that which one unworthier may attain,
And die with grieving.

PORTIA   You must take your chance,
And either not attempt to choose at all
Or swear before you choose, if you choose wrong
Never to speak to lady afterward
In way of marriage. Therefore be advised.

MOROCCO
Nor will not. Come, bring me unto my chance.   43

PORTIA
First, forward to the temple. After dinner   44
Your hazard shall be made.

MOROCCO   Good fortune then!
To make me blest or cursed'st among men.

                              [*Cornets, and*] *exeunt.*

                              ❖

2.2   *Enter* [*Launcelot*] *the Clown, alone.*

LAUNCELOT Certainly my conscience will serve me to 1
run from this Jew my master. The fiend is at mine
elbow and tempts me, saying to me, "Gobbo, Launcelot
Gobbo, good Launcelot," or "Good Gobbo," or "Good
Launcelot Gobbo, use your legs, take the start, run
away." My conscience says, "No, take heed, honest
Launcelot, take heed, honest Gobbo," or, as aforesaid,

---

27 o'erstare outstare   **30 'a** he   **32 Lichas** a page of Hercules (Alcides)
43 Nor will not i.e., nor indeed will I violate the oath   **44 to the
temple** i.e., in order to take the oaths

2.2. Location: Venice. A street.
1 serve permit

"honest Launcelot Gobbo, do not run; scorn running
with thy heels." Well, the most courageous fiend bids 9
me pack. "Fia!" says the fiend; "Away!" says the fiend. 10
"For the heavens, rouse up a brave mind," says the 11
fiend, "and run." Well, my conscience, hanging about 12
the neck of my heart, says very wisely to me, "My hon- 13
est friend Launcelot, being an honest man's son," or
rather an honest woman's son—for indeed my father
did something smack, something grow to, he had a 16
kind of taste—well, my conscience says, "Launcelot, 17
budge not." "Budge," says the fiend. "Budge not," says
my conscience. "Conscience," say I, "you counsel
well." "Fiend," say I, "you counsel well." To be ruled by
my conscience, I should stay with the Jew my master,
who, God bless the mark, is a kind of devil; and to run 22
away from the Jew, I should be ruled by the fiend, who,
saving your reverence, is the devil himself. Certainly
the Jew is the very devil incarnation; and, in my con- 25
science, my conscience is but a kind of hard conscience,
to offer to counsel me to stay with the Jew. The fiend
gives the more friendly counsel. I will run, fiend; my
heels are at your commandment; I will run.

Enter Old Gobbo, with a basket.

GOBBO Master young man, you, I pray you, which is 30
the way to master Jew's?
LAUNCELOT [*Aside*] O heavens, this is my true-
begotten father, who, being more than sand-blind, 33
high-gravel-blind, knows me not. I will try confusions 34
with him.
GOBBO Master young gentleman, I pray you, which is
the way to master Jew's?

9 with thy heels i.e., emphatically (with a pun on the literal sense)
10 pack begone. **Fia** i.e., via, away **11 For the heavens** i.e., in heaven's
name **12–13 hanging . . . heart** i.e., timidly **16–17 something . . . taste**
i.e., had a tendency to lechery **22 God . . . mark** (An expression by way
of apology for introducing something potentially offensive, as also in
saving your reverence.) **25 incarnation** (Launcelot means "incarnate.")
30 you (Gobbo uses the formal *you* but switches to the familiar
thou, l. 88, when he accepts Launcelot as his son.) **33 sand-blind** dim-
sighted **34 high-gravel-blind** blinder than sand-blind. (A term seemingly
invented by Launcelot.) **try confusions** (Launcelot's blunder for *try
conclusions*, i.e., experiment, though his error is comically apt.)

LAUNCELOT   Turn up on your right hand at the next turning, but at the next turning of all on your left; marry, at the very next turning, turn of no hand, but 40 turn down indirectly to the Jew's house.

GOBBO   By God's sonties, 'twill be a hard way to hit. 42 Can you tell me whether one Launcelot, that dwells with him, dwell with him or no?

LAUNCELOT   Talk you of young Master Launcelot? [*Aside.*] Mark me now; now will I raise the waters.— 46 Talk you of young Master Launcelot?

GOBBO   No master, sir, but a poor man's son. His father, 48 though I say 't, is an honest exceeding poor man and, God be thanked, well to live. 50

LAUNCELOT   Well, let his father be what 'a will, we talk 51 of young Master Launcelot.

GOBBO   Your worship's friend, and Launcelot, sir. 53

LAUNCELOT   But I pray you, ergo, old man, ergo, I be- 54 seech you, talk you of young Master Launcelot?

GOBBO   Of Launcelot, an 't please your mastership.

LAUNCELOT   Ergo, Master Launcelot. Talk not of Master Launcelot, Father, for the young gentleman, according 58 to Fates and Destinies and such odd sayings, the Sis- 59 ters Three and such branches of learning, is indeed 60 deceased, or, as you would say in plain terms, gone to heaven.

GOBBO   Marry, God forbid! The boy was the very staff of my age, my very prop.

LAUNCELOT   Do I look like a cudgel or a hovel post, a 65 staff, or a prop? Do you know me, Father?

GOBBO   Alack the day, I know you not, young gentle-man. But I pray you, tell me, is my boy, God rest his soul, alive or dead?

LAUNCELOT   Do you not know me, Father?

GOBBO   Alack, sir, I am sand-blind. I know you not.

---

40 marry i.e., by the Virgin Mary, indeed. (A mild interjection.)
42 sonties saints   **46 raise the waters** start tears   **48 master** (The title was applied to gentlefolk only.)   **50 well to live** enjoying a good liveli-hood. (Perhaps Old Gobbo intends the phrase to mean "in good health," since he protests that he is poor.)   **51 'a** he   **53 Your . . . Launcelot** (Again, Old Gobbo denies that Launcelot is entitled to be called "Mas-ter.")   **54 ergo** therefore (if it means anything)   **58 Father** (1) old man (2) Father   **59–60 the Sisters Three** the three Fates   **65 hovel post** sup-port for a hovel or open shed

LAUNCELOT Nay, indeed, if you had your eyes you
might fail of the knowing me; it is a wise father that 73
knows his own child. Well, old man, I will tell you 74
news of your son. [*He kneels.*] Give me your blessing;
truth will come to light; murder cannot be hid long; a
man's son may, but in the end truth will out.

GOBBO Pray you, sir, stand up. I am sure you are not
Launcelot, my boy.

LAUNCELOT Pray you, let's have no more fooling about
it, but give me your blessing. I am Launcelot, your 81
boy that was, your son that is, your child that shall be. 82

GOBBO I cannot think you are my son.

LAUNCELOT I know not what I shall think of that; but I
am Launcelot, the Jew's man, and I am sure Margery
your wife is my mother.

GOBBO Her name is Margery, indeed. I'll be sworn, if
thou be Launcelot, thou art mine own flesh and blood.
Lord worshiped might he be, what a beard hast thou 89
got! Thou hast got more hair on thy chin than Dobbin
my fill horse has on his tail. 91

LAUNCELOT [*Rising*] It should seem, then, that Dobbin's tail grows backward. I am sure he had more hair 93
of his tail than I have of my face when I last saw him. 94

GOBBO Lord, how art thou changed! How dost thou and
thy master agree? I have brought him a present. How
'gree you now?

LAUNCELOT Well, well; but for mine own part, as I
have set up my rest to run away, so I will not rest till 99
I have run some ground. My master's a very Jew. Give 100
him a present? Give him a halter! I am famished in his 101
service; you may tell every finger I have with my ribs. 102
Father, I am glad you are come. Give me your present 103

73–74 it is . . . child (Reverses the proverb "It is a wise child that knows
his own father.") **81–82 your . . . shall be** (Echoes the *Gloria* from the
Book of Common Prayer: "As it was in the beginning, is now, and ever
shall be.") **89 beard** (Stage tradition has Old Gobbo mistake Launcelot's long hair for a beard.) **91 fill horse** cart horse **93 grows backward** (1) grows inward, shorter (2) grows at the wrong end **94 of** in, on
99 set up my rest determined, risked all. (A metaphor from the card
game *primero*, in which a final wager is made.) **100 very** veritable
101 halter hangman's noose **102 tell** count. **tell . . . ribs** (Comically
reverses the usual saying of counting one's ribs with one's fingers.)
103 Give me give. (*Me* is used colloquially.)

to one Master Bassanio, who indeed gives rare new
liveries. If I serve not him, I will run as far as God has 105
any ground. O rare fortune, here comes the man! To
him, Father, for I am a Jew if I serve the Jew any longer.

*Enter Bassanio, with [Leonardo and] a follower
or two.*

BASSANIO You may do so, but let it be so hasted that 108
supper be ready at the farthest by five of the clock. See 109
these letters delivered, put the liveries to making, and
desire Gratiano to come anon to my lodging.
                                     [*Exit a Servant.*]
LAUNCELOT To him, Father.
GOBBO [*Advancing*] God bless your worship!
BASSANIO Gramercy. Wouldst thou aught with me?   114
GOBBO Here's my son, sir, a poor boy—
LAUNCELOT Not a poor boy, sir, but the rich Jew's man,
that would, sir, as my father shall specify—
GOBBO He hath a great infection, sir, as one would say, 118
to serve—
LAUNCELOT Indeed, the short and the long is, I serve
the Jew, and have a desire, as my father shall specify—
GOBBO His master and he, saving your worship's reverence, are scarce cater-cousins—   123
LAUNCELOT To be brief, the very truth is that the Jew,
having done me wrong, doth cause me, as my father,
being, I hope, an old man, shall frutify unto you—   126
GOBBO I have here a dish of doves that I would bestow
upon your worship, and my suit is—
LAUNCELOT In very brief, the suit is impertinent to my- 129
self, as your worship shall know by this honest old
man, and, though I say it, though old man, yet poor
man, my father.
BASSANIO One speak for both. What would you?
LAUNCELOT Serve you, sir.
GOBBO That is the very defect of the matter, sir.   135

---

105 liveries uniforms or costumes for servants   **108 hasted** hastened,
hurried   **109 farthest** latest   **114 Gramercy** many thanks.   **aught**
anything   **118 infection** (Blunder for *affection* or *inclination*.)
123 cater-cousins good friends   **126 frutify** (Launcelot may be trying to
say "fructify," but he means "certify" or "notify.")   **129 impertinent**
(Blunder for *pertinent*.)   **135 defect** (Blunder for *effect*, i.e., "purport.")

BASSANIO
  I know thee well; thou hast obtained thy suit.
  Shylock thy master spoke with me this day,
  And hath preferred thee, if it be preferment   138
  To leave a rich Jew's service to become
  The follower of so poor a gentleman.

LAUNCELOT   The old proverb is very well parted be-   141
tween my master Shylock and you, sir: you have the
grace of God, sir, and he hath enough.

BASSANIO
  Thou speak'st it well. Go, father, with thy son.
  Take leave of thy old master, and inquire
  My lodging out. [*To a Servant.*] Give him a livery
  More guarded than his fellows'. See it done.   147

LAUNCELOT   Father, in. I cannot get a service, no! I have
ne'er a tongue in my head, well! [*Looks at his palm.*] If
any man in Italy have a fairer table which doth offer to   150
swear upon a book, I shall have good fortune. Go to,
here's a simple linc of life. Here's a small trifle of
wives! Alas, fifteen wives is nothing. Eleven widows
and nine maids is a simple coming-in for one man.   154
And then to scape drowning thrice, and to be in peril
of my life with the edge of a feather bed! Here are   156
simple scapes. Well, if Fortune be a woman, she's a   157
good wench for this gear. Father, come, I'll take my   158
leave of the Jew in the twinkling.

                Exit Clown [*with Old Gobbo*].

BASSANIO
  I pray thee, good Leonardo, think on this:
                [*Giving him a list*]
  These things being bought and orderly bestowed,
  Return in haste, for I do feast tonight   162
  My best-esteemed acquaintance. Hie thee, go.

LEONARDO
  My best endeavors shall be done herein.
                [*He starts to leave.*]

138 preferred recommended   **141 proverb** i.e., "He who has the grace
of God has enough"   **147 guarded** trimmed with braided ornament
150 table palm of the hand. (Launcelot now reads the lines of his
palm.)   **154 simple coming-in** modest income (with sexual suggestion)
156 feather bed (suggesting marriage bed or love bed; Launcelot sees
sexual adventure in his palm reading)   **157 Fortune . . . woman** (Fortune
was personified as a goddess.)   **158 gear** matter   **162 feast** give a feast for

Enter Gratiano.

GRATIANO
  Where's your master?
LEONARDO   Yonder, sir, he walks.
                                    Exit Leonardo.
GRATIANO   Signor Bassanio!
BASSANIO   Gratiano!
GRATIANO
  I have a suit to you.
BASSANIO   You have obtained it.
GRATIANO   You must not deny me. I must go with you
  to Belmont.
BASSANIO
  Why, then you must. But hear thee, Gratiano;
  Thou art too wild, too rude and bold of voice—
  Parts that become thee happily enough,   173
  And in such eyes as ours appear not faults,
  But where thou art not known, why, there they show
  Something too liberal. Pray thee, take pain   176
  To allay with some cold drops of modesty   177
  Thy skipping spirit, lest through thy wild behavior
  I be misconstered in the place I go to   179
  And lose my hopes.
GRATIANO   Signor Bassanio, hear me:
  If I do not put on a sober habit,
  Talk with respect and swear but now and then,
  Wear prayer books in my pocket, look demurely,
  Nay more, while grace is saying, hood mine eyes   184
  Thus with my hat, and sigh and say "amen,"
  Use all the observance of civility,
  Like one well studied in a sad ostent   187
  To please his grandam, never trust me more.
BASSANIO   Well, we shall see your bearing.
GRATIANO
  Nay, but I bar tonight. You shall not gauge me
  By what we do tonight.
BASSANIO   No, that were pity.
  I would entreat you rather to put on

173 Parts qualities   **176 liberal** free of manner (often with sexual connotation)   **177 allay** temper, moderate   **179 misconstered** misconstrued
184 saying being said   **187 sad ostent** grave appearance

Your boldest suit of mirth, for we have friends
That purpose merriment. But fare you well;
I have some business.

GRATIANO
And I must to Lorenzo and the rest,
But we will visit you at suppertime.   *Exeunt.*

✢

2.3   *Enter Jessica and [Launcelot] the Clown.*

JESSICA
I am sorry thou wilt leave my father so.
Our house is hell, and thou, a merry devil,
Didst rob it of some taste of tediousness.
But fare thee well; there is a ducat for thee.
                                    [Giving money.]
And, Launcelot, soon at supper shalt thou see
Lorenzo, who is thy new master's guest.
Give him this letter; do it secretly.   *[Giving a letter.]*
And so farewell; I would not have my father
See me in talk with thee.

LAUNCELOT   Adieu! Tears exhibit my tongue. Most 10
beautiful pagan, most sweet Jew! If a Christian did not
play the knave and get thee, I am much deceived. But, 12
adieu! These foolish drops do something drown my
manly spirit. Adieu!

JESSICA   Farewell, good Launcelot.   *[Exit Launcelot.]*
Alack, what heinous sin is it in me
To be ashamed to be my father's child!
But though I am a daughter to his blood,
I am not to his manners. O Lorenzo,
If thou keep promise, I shall end this strife,
Become a Christian and thy loving wife.   *Exit.*

✢

2.3. **Location: Venice. Shylock's house.**
10 **exhibit** (Blunder for *inhibit*, "restrain.")   12 **get** beget

2.4 *Enter Gratiano, Lorenzo, Salerio, and Solanio.*

LORENZO
  Nay, we will slink away in suppertime,   1
  Disguise us at my lodging, and return
  All in an hour.

GRATIANO
  We have not made good preparation.

SALERIO
  We have not spoke us yet of torchbearers.   5

SOLANIO
  'Tis vile, unless it may be quaintly ordered,   6
  And better in my mind not undertook.

LORENZO
  'Tis now but four o'clock. We have two hours
  To furnish us.

    Enter Launcelot [with a letter].

          Friend Launcelot, what's the news?

LAUNCELOT An it shall please you to break up this, it 10
shall seem to signify.   *[Giving the letter.]*

LORENZO
  I know the hand. In faith, 'tis a fair hand,
  And whiter than the paper it writ on
  Is the fair hand that writ.

GRATIANO   Love news, in faith.

LAUNCELOT By your leave, sir.   *[He starts to leave.]*

LORENZO Whither goest thou?

LAUNCELOT Marry, sir, to bid my old master the Jew to
sup tonight with my new master the Christian.

LORENZO
  Hold here, take this. *[He gives money.]* Tell gentle Jessica
  I will not fail her; speak it privately.

              Exit Clown [Launcelot].

  Go, gentlemen,
  Will you prepare you for this masque tonight?
  I am provided of a torchbearer.

2.4. Location: Venice. A street.
1 in during **5 spoke . . . of** yet bespoken, ordered **6 quaintly ordered**
skillfully and tastefully managed **10 An** if. **break up** i.e., open the
seal. (Literally, a term from carving.)

SALERIO
  Ay, marry, I'll be gone about it straight.
SOLANIO
  And so will I.
LORENZO   Meet me and Gratiano
  At Gratiano's lodging some hour hence.
SALERIO   'Tis good we do so.   *Exit [with Solanio].*
GRATIANO
  Was not that letter from fair Jessica?
LORENZO
  I must needs tell thee all. She hath directed
  How I shall take her from her father's house,
  What gold and jewels she is furnished with,
  What page's suit she hath in readiness.
  If e'er the Jew her father come to heaven,
  It will be for his gentle daughter's sake;   34
  And never dare Misfortune cross her foot,   35
  Unless she do it under this excuse,   36
  That she is issue to a faithless Jew.   37
  Come, go with me; peruse this as thou goest.
                    [He gives Gratiano the letter.]
  Fair Jessica shall be my torchbearer.   *Exeunt.*

✢

2.5   *Enter [Shylock the] Jew and [Launcelot,] his*
          man that was, the Clown.

SHYLOCK
  Well, thou shalt see, thy eyes shall be thy judge,
  The difference of old Shylock and Bassanio.—   2
  What, Jessica!—Thou shalt not gormandize,   3
  As thou hast done with me—What, Jessica!—
  And sleep and snore, and rend apparel out—   5
  Why, Jessica, I say!
LAUNCELOT   Why, Jessica!

34 **gentle** (with pun on *gentile?*)   35 **foot** footpath   36 **she**
i.e., Misfortune   37 **she is issue** i.e., Jessica is child.   **faithless**
pagan

2.5. Location: Venice. Before Shylock's house.
2 **of** between   3 **gormandize** eat gluttonously   5 **rend apparel out** i.e.,
wear out your clothes

SHYLOCK
  Who bids thee call? I do not bid thee call.
LAUNCELOT   Your worship was wont to tell me I could
  do nothing without bidding.

    Enter Jessica.

JESSICA   Call you? What is your will?
SHYLOCK
  I am bid forth to supper, Jessica.
  There are my keys. But wherefore should I go?
  I am not bid for love—they flatter me—
  But yet I'll go in hate, to feed upon
  The prodigal Christian. Jessica, my girl,
  Look to my house. I am right loath to go.   17
  There is some ill a-brewing towards my rest,
  For I did dream of moneybags tonight.   19
LAUNCELOT   I beseech you, sir, go. My young master
  doth expect your reproach.   21
SHYLOCK   So do I his.
LAUNCELOT   And they have conspired together. I will
  not say you shall see a masque, but if you do, then it
  was not for nothing that my nose fell a-bleeding on
  Black Monday last at six o'clock i' the morning, falling   26
  out that year on Ash Wednesday was four year in th'
  afternoon.
SHYLOCK
  What, are there masques? Hear you me, Jessica:
  Lock up my doors, and when you hear the drum
  And the vile squealing of the wry-necked fife,   31
  Clamber not you up to the casements then,
  Nor thrust your head into the public street
  To gaze on Christian fools with varnished faces,   34
  But stop my house's ears, I mean my casements.
  Let not the sound of shallow foppery enter
  My sober house. By Jacob's staff I swear   37

17 **right loath** reluctant   19 **tonight** last night   21 **reproach** (Launcelot's blunder for *approach.* Shylock takes it in grim humor.)   26 **Black
Monday** Easter Monday. (So called, according to Stow, because of a cold
and stormy Easter Monday when Edward III was besieging Paris. Launcelot's talk of omens is perhaps intentional gibberish, a parody of Shylock's fears.)   31 **wry-necked** i.e., played with the musician's head awry;
or, on an instrument with the head twisted awry   34 **varnished faces** i.e.,
painted masks   37 **Jacob's staff** (See Genesis 32:10 and Hebrews 11:21.)

I have no mind of feasting forth tonight.
But I will go. Go you before me, sirrah;
Say I will come.

LAUNCELOT   I will go before, sir. [*To Jessica.*] Mistress,
look out at window, for all this;
        There will come a Christian by,
        Will be worth a Jewess' eye.   [*Exit.*]

SHYLOCK
What says that fool of Hagar's offspring, ha?   45

JESSICA
His words were "Farewell, mistress," nothing else.

SHYLOCK
The patch is kind enough, but a huge feeder,   47
Snail-slow in profit, and he sleeps by day   48
More than the wildcat. Drones hive not with me;
Therefore I part with him, and part with him
To one that I would have him help to waste
His borrowed purse. Well, Jessica, go in.
Perhaps I will return immediately.
Do as I bid you; shut doors after you.
Fast bind, fast find—   55
A proverb never stale in thrifty mind.   *Exit.*

JESSICA
Farewell, and if my fortune be not crossed,
I have a father, you a daughter, lost.   *Exit.*

❖

2.6   *Enter the maskers, Gratiano and Salerio.*

GRATIANO
This is the penthouse under which Lorenzo   1
Desired us to make stand.

SALERIO   His hour is almost past.

GRATIANO
And it is marvel he outdwells his hour,   4

---

45 Hagar's offspring (Hagar, a gentile and Abraham's servant, gave
birth to Ishmael; both mother and son were cast out after the birth of
Isaac.) **47 patch** fool **48 profit** profitable labor **55 Fast . . . find** i.e.,
something firmly secured or bound will always be easily located

2.6. Location: Before Shylock's house, as in scene 5.
1 penthouse projecting roof from a house **4 it . . . hour** i.e., it is sur-
prising that he is late

For lovers ever run before the clock.

SALERIO
O, ten times faster Venus' pigeons fly   6
To seal love's bonds new-made than they are wont
To keep obligèd faith unforfeited!   8

GRATIANO
That ever holds. Who riseth from a feast
With that keen appetite that he sits down?
Where is the horse that doth untread again   11
His tedious measures with the unbated fire
That he did pace them first? All things that are,
Are with more spirit chasèd than enjoyed.
How like a younger or a prodigal   15
The scarfèd bark puts from her native bay,   16
Hugged and embracèd by the strumpet wind!   17
How like the prodigal doth she return,
With overweathered ribs and ragged sails,   19
Lean, rent, and beggared by the strumpet wind! 20

        Enter Lorenzo, [masked].

SALERIO
Here comes Lorenzo. More of this hereafter.

LORENZO
Sweet friends, your patience for my long abode; 22
Not I, but my affairs, have made you wait.
When you shall please to play the thieves for wives,
I'll watch as long for you then. Approach;
Here dwells my father Jew. Ho! Who's within?   26

        [Enter] Jessica, above [in boy's clothes].

JESSICA
Who are you? Tell me for more certainty,
Albeit I'll swear that I do know your tongue.

LORENZO   Lorenzo, and thy love.

6 **Venus' pigeons** the doves that drew Venus' chariot   8 **obligèd** bound
by marriage or engagement.   **unforfeited** unbroken   11 **untread** re-
trace   15 **younger** i.e., younger son, as in the parable of the Prodigal
Son (Luke 15). (Often emended to *younker*, youth.)   16 **scarfèd** decorated
with flags or streamers   17 **strumpet** i.e., inconsistent, variable. (Refers
metaphorically to the harlots with whom the Prodigal Son wasted his
fortune.)   19 **overweathered** weatherbeaten   20 **rent** torn   22 **your patience** i.e., I beg your patience.   **abode** delay   26 **father** i.e., father-in-law

JESSICA
  Lorenzo, certain, and my love indeed,
  For who love I so much? And now who knows
  But you, Lorenzo, whether I am yours?

LORENZO
  Heaven and thy thoughts are witness that thou art.

JESSICA [*Throwing down a casket*]
  Here, catch this casket; it is worth the pains.
  I am glad 'tis night, you do not look on me,
  For I am much ashamed of my exchange.   36
  But love is blind, and lovers cannot see
  The pretty follies that themselves commit,   38
  For if they could, Cupid himself would blush
  To see me thus transformèd to a boy.

LORENZO
  Descend, for you must be my torchbearer.

JESSICA
  What, must I hold a candle to my shames?   42
  They in themselves, good sooth, are too too light.   43
  Why, 'tis an office of discovery, love,   44
  And I should be obscured.

LORENZO   So are you, sweet,
  Even in the lovely garnish of a boy.   46
  But come at once,
  For the close night doth play the runaway,   48
  And we are stayed for at Bassanio's feast.   49

JESSICA
  I will make fast the doors, and gild myself   50
  With some more ducats, and be with you straight.
                                    [*Exit above.*]

GRATIANO
  Now, by my hood, a gentle and no Jew.   52

LORENZO
  Beshrew me but I love her heartily,   53
  For she is wise, if I can judge of her,

36 exchange change of clothes   **38 pretty** ingenious, artful   **42 hold a candle** stand by and witness (with a play on the idea of acting as torchbearer)   **43 light** immodest (with pun on literal meaning)   **44 'tis . . . discovery** i.e., torchbearing is intended to shed light on matters   **46 garnish** outfit, trimmings   **48 close** dark.   **doth . . . runaway** i.e., is quickly passing   **49 stayed** waited   **50 gild** adorn. (Literally, cover with gold.)   **52 gentle** (with pun on *gentile*, as at 2.4.34)   **53 Beshrew** i.e., a mischief on. (A mild oath.)

And fair she is, if that mine eyes be true,
And true she is, as she hath proved herself;
And therefore, like herself—wise, fair, and true—
Shall she be placèd in my constant soul.

    Enter Jessica [below].

What, art thou come? On, gentlemen, away!
Our masking mates by this time for us stay.
             Exit [with Jessica and Salerio;
             Gratiano is about to follow them].

    Enter Antonio.

ANTONIO Who's there?
GRATIANO Signor Antonio?
ANTONIO
Fie, fie, Gratiano! Where are all the rest?
'Tis nine o'clock; our friends all stay for you.
No masque tonight. The wind is come about;
Bassanio presently will go aboard.
I have sent twenty out to seek for you.
GRATIANO
I am glad on 't. I desire no more delight
Than to be under sail and gone tonight.   *Exeunt.*

❖

2.7 *[Flourish of cornets.] Enter Portia, with [the
Prince of] Morocco, and both their trains.*

PORTIA
Go draw aside the curtains and discover   1
The several caskets to this noble prince.
           [The curtains are drawn.]
Now make your choice.
MOROCCO
The first, of gold, who this inscription bears,
"Who chooseth me shall gain what many men desire";
The second, silver, which this promise carries,
"Who chooseth me shall get as much as he deserves";
This third, dull lead, with warning all as blunt,

2.7. Location: Belmont. Portia's house.
1 discover reveal

"Who chooseth me must give and hazard all he hath."
How shall I know if I do choose the right?

PORTIA
The one of them contains my picture, Prince.
If you choose that, then I am yours withal.

MOROCCO
Some god direct my judgment! Let me see.
I will survey th' inscriptions back again.
What says this leaden casket?
"Who chooseth me must give and hazard all he hath."
Must give—for what? For lead? Hazard for lead?
This casket threatens. Men that hazard all
Do it in hope of fair advantages.
A golden mind stoops not to shows of dross;   20
I'll then nor give nor hazard aught for lead.   21
What says the silver with her virgin hue?
"Who chooseth me shall get as much as he deserves."
As much as he deserves! Pause there, Morocco,
And weigh thy value with an even hand.
If thou be'st rated by thy estimation,   26
Thou dost deserve enough; and yet enough
May not extend so far as to the lady;
And yet to be afeard of my deserving
Were but a weak disabling of myself.   30
As much as I deserve? Why, that's the lady.
I do in birth deserve her, and in fortunes,
In graces, and in qualities of breeding;
But more than these, in love I do deserve.
What if I strayed no farther, but chose here?
Let's see once more this saying graved in gold:
"Who chooseth me shall gain what many men desire."
Why, that's the lady; all the world desires her.
From the four corners of the earth they come
To kiss this shrine, this mortal breathing saint.
The Hyrcanian deserts and the vasty wilds   41
Of wide Arabia are as throughfares now

---

20 dross worthless matter. (Literally, the impurities cast off in the
melting down of metals.)   **21 nor give** neither give   **26 estimation**
valuation   **30 disabling** underrating   **41 Hyrcanian** (Hyrcania was the
country south of the Caspian Sea celebrated for its wildness.)

For princes to come view fair Portia.
The watery kingdom, whose ambitious head
Spits in the face of heaven, is no bar
To stop the foreign spirits, but they come,
As o'er a brook, to see fair Portia.
One of these three contains her heavenly picture.
Is 't like that lead contains her? 'Twere damnation
To think so base a thought; it were too gross
To rib her cerecloth in the obscure grave.   51
Or shall I think in silver she's immured,   52
Being ten times undervalued to tried gold?   53
O, sinful thought! Never so rich a gem
Was set in worse than gold. They have in England
A coin that bears the figure of an angel   56
Stamped in gold, but that's insculped upon;   57
But here an angel in a golden bed
Lies all within. Deliver me the key.
Here do I choose, and thrive I as I may!

PORTIA
There, take it, Prince; and if my form lie there,
Then I am yours.   [*He unlocks the golden casket.*]
MOROCCO   O hell! What have we here?
A carrion Death, within whose empty eye   63
There is a written scroll! I'll read the writing.
[*Reads.*] "All that glisters is not gold;
         Often have you heard that told.
         Many a man his life hath sold
         But my outside to behold.
         Gilded tombs do worms infold.
         Had you been as wise as bold,
         Young in limbs, in judgment old,
         Your answer had not been enscrolled.   72
         Fare you well; your suit is cold."
   Cold, indeed, and labor lost.
   Then, farewell, heat, and welcome, frost!

---

51 rib i.e., enclose. **cerecloth** wax cloth used in wrapping for burial
52 immured enclosed, confined **53 Being . . . to** which has only one
tenth of the value of **56 coin** i.e., the gold coin known as the *angel*,
which bore the device of the archangel Michael treading on the
dragon **57 insculped upon** merely engraved upon the surface
63 carrion Death death's-head **72 enscrolled** i.e., written on this scroll

Portia, adieu. I have too grieved a heart
To take a tedious leave. Thus losers part.
                    Exit [with his train. Flourish of cornets].
PORTIA
A gentle riddance. Draw the curtains, go.
Let all of his complexion choose me so.   79
                    [The curtains are closed, and] Exeunt.

✤

2.8   *Enter Salerio and Solanio.*

SALERIO
Why, man, I saw Bassanio under sail.
With him is Gratiano gone along,
And in their ship I am sure Lorenzo is not.
SOLANIO
The villain Jew with outcries raised the Duke,
Who went with him to search Bassanio's ship.
SALERIO
He came too late; the ship was under sail.
But there the Duke was given to understand
That in a gondola were seen together
Lorenzo and his amorous Jessica.
Besides, Antonio certified the Duke
They were not with Bassanio in his ship.
SOLANIO
I never heard a passion so confused,
So strange, outrageous, and so variable
As the dog Jew did utter in the streets:
"My daughter! O, my ducats! O, my daughter!
Fled with a Christian! O, my Christian ducats!
Justice! The law! My ducats, and my daughter!
A sealèd bag, two sealèd bags of ducats,
Of double ducats, stol'n from me by my daughter!
And jewels, two stones, two rich and precious stones,
Stol'n by my daughter! Justice! Find the girl!
She hath the stones upon her, and the ducats."

79 complexion temperament (not merely skin color)

2.8. Location: Venice. A street.

SALERIO

Why, all the boys in Venice follow him,
Crying, his stones, his daughter, and his ducats.

SOLANIO

Let good Antonio look he keep his day,   25
Or he shall pay for this.

SALERIO   Marry, well remembered.

I reasoned with a Frenchman yesterday,   27
Who told me, in the narrow seas that part   28
The French and English, there miscarried
A vessel of our country richly fraught.   30
I thought upon Antonio when he told me,
And wished in silence that it were not his.

SOLANIO

You were best to tell Antonio what you hear.
Yet do not suddenly, for it may grieve him.

SALERIO

A kinder gentleman treads not the earth.
I saw Bassanio and Antonio part.
Bassanio told him he would make some speed
Of his return; he answered, "Do not so.
Slubber not business for my sake, Bassanio,   39
But stay the very riping of the time;   40
And for the Jew's bond which he hath of me,   41
Let it not enter in your mind of love.
Be merry, and employ your chiefest thoughts
To courtship and such fair ostents of love   44
As shall conveniently become you there."
And even there, his eye being big with tears,   46
Turning his face, he put his hand behind him,
And with affection wondrous sensible   48
He wrung Bassanio's hand; and so they parted.

SOLANIO

I think he only loves the world for him.
I pray thee, let us go and find him out

---

25 look . . . day see to it that he repays his loan on time   **27 reasoned**
talked   **28 narrow seas** English Channel   **30 fraught** freighted
39 Slubber do hastily and badly   **40 But . . . time** i.e., pursue your
business at Belmont until it is brought to completion   **41 for** as for
44 ostents expressions, shows   **46 there** thereupon, then   **48 sensible**
strongly evident

And quicken his embracèd heaviness   52
With some delight or other.

SALERIO   Do we so.   *Exeunt.*

❖

2.9   *Enter Nerissa and a Servitor.*

NERISSA
Quick, quick, I pray thee, draw the curtain straight.   1
                         [*The curtains are drawn.*]
The Prince of Aragon hath ta'en his oath,
And comes to his election presently.   3

    [*Flourish of cornets.*] *Enter* [*the Prince of*]
    Aragon, his train, and Portia.

PORTIA
Behold, there stand the caskets, noble Prince.
If you choose that wherein I am contained,
Straight shall our nuptial rites be solemnized;
But if you fail, without more speech, my lord,
You must be gone from hence immediately.

ARAGON
I am enjoined by oath to observe three things:
First, never to unfold to anyone
Which casket 'twas I chose; next, if I fail
Of the right casket, never in my life
To woo a maid in way of marriage;
Lastly,
If I do fail in fortune of my choice,
Immediately to leave you and be gone.

PORTIA
To these injunctions everyone doth swear
That comes to hazard for my worthless self.

ARAGON
And so have I addressed me. Fortune now   19
To my heart's hope! Gold, silver, and base lead.

52 **quicken . . . heaviness** lighten the sorrow he has embraced

2.9. Location: Belmont. Portia's house.
s.d. **Servitor** servant   1 **straight** at once   3 **election** choice.   **presently**
immediately   19 **addressed me** prepared myself (by this swearing)

"Who chooseth me must give and hazard all he hath."
You shall look fairer ere I give or hazard.
What says the golden chest? Ha, let me see:
"Who chooseth me shall gain what many men desire."
What many men desire! That "many" may be meant   25
By the fool multitude that choose by show,
Not learning more than the fond eye doth teach,   27
Which pries not to th' interior, but like the martlet   28
Builds in the weather on the outward wall,   29
Even in the force and road of casualty.   30
I will not choose what many men desire,
Because I will not jump with common spirits   32
And rank me with the barbarous multitudes.
Why then, to thee, thou silver treasure-house!
Tell me once more what title thou dost bear:
"Who chooseth me shall get as much as he deserves."
And well said too; for who shall go about
To cozen fortune and be honorable   38
Without the stamp of merit? Let none presume   39
To wear an undeservèd dignity.
O, that estates, degrees, and offices   41
Were not derived corruptly, and that clear honor
Were purchased by the merit of the wearer!
How many then should cover that stand bare?   44
How many be commanded that command?   45
How much low peasantry would then be gleaned   46
From the true seed of honor, and how much honor   47
Picked from the chaff and ruin of the times
To be new-varnished? Well, but to my choice: 49
"Who chooseth me shall get as much as he deserves."
I will assume desert. Give me a key for this,
And instantly unlock my fortunes here.

[*He opens the silver casket.*]

---

25 meant interpreted   **27 fond** foolish   **28 martlet** swift   **29 in** exposed
to   **30 force . . . casualty** power and path of mischance   **32 jump**
agree   **38 cozen** cheat   **39 stamp** seal of approval   **41 estates, degrees**
status, social rank   **44 cover . . . bare** i.e., wear hats (of authority) who
now stand bareheaded   **45 How . . . command** how many then should
be servants that are now masters   **46 gleaned** culled out   **47 the true
seed of honor** i.e., persons of noble descent   **49 new-varnished** i.e.,
having the luster of their true nobility restored to them

PORTIA
  Too long a pause for that which you find there.
ARAGON
  What's here? The portrait of a blinking idiot,
  Presenting me a schedule! I will read it.   55
  How much unlike art thou to Portia!
  How much unlike my hopes and my deservings!
  "Who chooseth me shall have as much as he deserves."
  Did I deserve no more than a fool's head?
  Is that my prize? Are my deserts no better?
PORTIA
  To offend and judge are distinct offices   61
  And of opposèd natures.
ARAGON   What is here?   62
  [*Reads*.] "The fire seven times tried this;   63
            Seven times tried that judgment is
            That did never choose amiss.
            Some there be that shadows kiss;
            Such have but a shadow's bliss.
            There be fools alive, iwis,   68
            Silvered o'er, and so was this.   69
            Take what wife you will to bed,
            I will ever be your head.   71
            So begone; you are sped."   72

            Still more fool I shall appear   73
            By the time I linger here.   74
            With one fool's head I came to woo,
            But I go away with two.
            Sweet, adieu. I'll keep my oath,
            Patiently to bear my wroth.   78
                          [*Exeunt Aragon and train.*]
PORTIA
  Thus hath the candle singed the moth.

---

55 schedule written paper   **61–62 To offend . . . natures** i.e., you have
no right, having submitted your case to judgment, to attempt to judge
your own case   **63 tried** tested, purified (?)   **this** i.e., the wise sayings on
the scroll (that have often been proved right by hard experience)
68 iwis certainly   **69 Silvered o'er** i.e., with silver hair and so apparently wise   **71 I . . . head** i.e., you will always have a fool's head
72 sped done for   **73–74 Still . . . here** i.e., I shall seem all the greater
fool for wasting any more time here   **78 wroth** sorrow, unhappy lot. (A
variant of *ruth*.)

O, these deliberate fools! When they do choose,   80
They have the wisdom by their wit to lose.

NERISSA
The ancient saying is no heresy:
Hanging and wiving goes by destiny.

PORTIA   Come, draw the curtain, Nerissa.

                          [*The curtains are closed.*]

        Enter Messenger.

MESSENGER
Where is my lady?

PORTIA   Here. What would my lord?   85

MESSENGER
Madam, there is alighted at your gate
A young Venetian, one that comes before
To signify th' approaching of his lord,
From whom he bringeth sensible regreets,   89
To wit, besides commends and courteous breath,   90
Gifts of rich value. Yet I have not seen   91
So likely an ambassador of love.   92
A day in April never came so sweet
To show how costly summer was at hand   94
As this fore-spurrer comes before his lord.   95

PORTIA
No more, I pray thee. I am half afeard
Thou wilt say anon he is some kin to thee,
Thou spend'st such high-day wit in praising him.   98
Come, come, Nerissa, for I long to see
Quick Cupid's post that comes so mannerly.   100

NERISSA
Bassanio, Lord Love, if thy will it be!   *Exeunt.*

❧

80 deliberate reasoning, calculating   **85 my lord** (A jesting response to
"my lady.")   **89 sensible regreets** tangible gifts, greetings   **90 commends** greetings. **breath** speech   **91 Yet** heretofore   **92 likely**
promising   **94 costly** lavish, rich   **95 fore-spurrer** herald, harbinger
98 high-day holiday (i.e., extravagant)   **100 post** messenger

3.1   [*Enter*] *Solanio and Salerio.*

SOLANIO   Now, what news on the Rialto?

SALERIO   Why, yet it lives there unchecked that Antonio 2
hath a ship of rich lading wrecked on the narrow 3
seas—the Goodwins, I think they call the place, a very 4
dangerous flat, and fatal, where the carcasses of many 5
a tall ship lie buried, as they say, if my gossip Report 6
be an honest woman of her word.

SOLANIO   I would she were as lying a gossip in that as
ever knapped ginger or made her neighbors believe 9
she wept for the death of a third husband. But it is
true, without any slips of prolixity or crossing the 11
plain highway of talk, that the good Antonio, the hon- 12
est Antonio—O, that I had a title good enough to keep
his name company!—

SALERIO   Come, the full stop.   15

SOLANIO   Ha, what sayest thou? Why, the end is, he
hath lost a ship.

SALERIO   I would it might prove the end of his losses.

SOLANIO   Let me say "amen" betimes, lest the devil 19
cross my prayer, for here he comes in the likeness of 20
a Jew.

Enter Shylock.

How now, Shylock, what news among the merchants?

SHYLOCK   You knew, none so well, none so well as you,
of my daughter's flight.

SALERIO   That's certain. I for my part knew the tailor
that made the wings she flew withal.   26

SOLANIO   And Shylock for his own part knew the bird

3.1. Location: Venice. A street.
2 unchecked undenied   **3–4 the narrow seas** the English Channel, as at
2.8.28.   **4 Goodwins** Goodwin Sands, off the Kentish coast near the
Thames estuary   **5 flat** shoal, sandbank   **6 gossip Report** i.e., Dame
Rumor   **9 knapped** nibbled   **11 slips of prolixity** lapses into long-
windedness; or, longwinded lies   **11–12 crossing . . . talk** deviating
from honest plain speech   **15 Come . . . stop** finish your story   **19 be-**
times while there is yet time   **20 cross** thwart   **26 wings** i.e., the
boy's clothes in which she fled. Jessica's flight is compared to a bird's
(cf. ll. 27–28), but *wings* is also a tailor's word to describe an ornamen-
tal flap near the shoulder of a garment.

was fledge, and then it is the complexion of them all   28
to leave the dam.   29

SHYLOCK   She is damned for it.

SALERIO   That's certain, if the devil may be her judge.

SHYLOCK   My own flesh and blood to rebel!

SOLANIO   Out upon it, old carrion! Rebels it at these   33
years?   34

SHYLOCK   I say, my daughter is my flesh and my blood.

SALERIO   There is more difference between thy flesh and
hers than between jet and ivory, more between your   37
bloods than there is between red wine and Rhenish.   38
But tell us, do you hear whether Antonio have had
any loss at sea or no?

SHYLOCK   There I have another bad match! A bankrupt,   41
a prodigal, who dare scarce show his head on the
Rialto; a beggar, that was used to come so smug upon
the mart! Let him look to his bond. He was wont to
call me usurer. Let him look to his bond. He was wont
to lend money for a Christian courtesy. Let him look to
his bond.

SALERIO   Why, I am sure, if he forfeit, thou wilt not take
his flesh. What's that good for?

SHYLOCK   To bait fish withal. If it will feed nothing else,   50
it will feed my revenge. He hath disgraced me, and
hindered me half a million, laughed at my losses,
mocked at my gains, scorned my nation, thwarted my
bargains, cooled my friends, heated mine enemies;
and what's his reason? I am a Jew. Hath not a Jew
eyes? Hath not a Jew hands, organs, dimensions,
senses, affections, passions? Fed with the same food,
hurt with the same weapons, subject to the same dis-
eases, healed by the same means, warmed and cooled
by the same winter and summer, as a Christian is? If
you prick us, do we not bleed? If you tickle us, do we
not laugh? If you poison us, do we not die? And if you
wrong us, shall we not revenge? If we are like you in

28 fledge ready to fly.   **complexion** natural disposition   **29 dam**
mother   **33–34 Rebels . . . years** (Solanio pretends to interpret Shylock's
cry about the rebellion of his own flesh and blood as referring to his
own carnal desires.)   **37 jet** a hard form of coal capable of taking a
brilliant polish   **38 Rhenish** i.e., a German white wine from the Rhine
valley   **41 match** bargain   **50 To bait** to lure, to act as bait for

the rest, we will resemble you in that. If a Jew wrong
a Christian, what is his humility? Revenge. If a Chris- 65
tian wrong a Jew, what should his sufferance be by 66
Christian example? Why, revenge. The villainy you
teach me I will execute, and it shall go hard but I will
better the instruction.

Enter a Man from Antonio.

MAN   Gentlemen, my master Antonio is at his house
and desires to speak with you both.

SALERIO   We have been up and down to seek him.

Enter Tubal.

SOLANIO   Here comes another of the tribe. A third cannot be matched, unless the devil himself turn Jew.   74

Exeunt gentlemen [Solanio, Salerio, with Man].

SHYLOCK   How now, Tubal, what news from Genoa?
Hast thou found my daughter?

TUBAL   I often came where I did hear of her, but cannot
find her.

SHYLOCK   Why, there, there, there, there! A diamond
gone, cost me two thousand ducats in Frankfort! The
curse never fell upon our nation till now; I never felt it
till now. Two thousand ducats in that, and other precious, precious jewels. I would my daughter were
dead at my foot, and the jewels in her ear! Would she
were hearsed at my foot, and the ducats in her coffin! 85
No news of them? Why, so—and I know not what's
spent in the search. Why, thou loss upon loss! The
thief gone with so much, and so much to find the
thief, and no satisfaction, no revenge! Nor no ill luck
stirring but what lights o' my shoulders, no sighs but
o' my breathing, no tears but o' my shedding.

TUBAL   Yes, other men have ill luck too. Antonio, as I
heard in Genoa—

SHYLOCK   What, what, what? Ill luck, ill luck?

TUBAL   —hath an argosy cast away, coming from Tripolis.

SHYLOCK   I thank God, I thank God. Is it true, is it true?

TUBAL   I spoke with some of the sailors that escaped the
wreck.

65–66 his . . . his the Christian's . . . the Jew's   **74 matched** i.e., found to
match them   **85 hearsed** coffined

SHYLOCK   I thank thee, good Tubal. Good news, good
news! Ha, ha! Heard in Genoa?

TUBAL   Your daughter spent in Genoa, as I heard, one
night fourscore ducats.

SHYLOCK   Thou stick'st a dagger in me. I shall never see
my gold again. Fourscore ducats at a sitting, fourscore
ducats!

TUBAL   There came divers of Antonio's creditors in my
company to Venice that swear he cannot choose but
break.   108

SHYLOCK   I am very glad of it. I'll plague him, I'll torture
him. I am glad of it.

TUBAL   One of them showed me a ring that he had of
your daughter for a monkey.

SHYLOCK   Out upon her! Thou torturest me, Tubal. It
was my turquoise; I had it of Leah when I was a bach-   114
elor. I would not have given it for a wilderness of
monkeys.

TUBAL   But Antonio is certainly undone.

SHYLOCK   Nay, that's true, that's very true. Go, Tubal,
fee me an officer; bespeak him a fortnight before. I will   119
have the heart of him if he forfeit, for were he out of
Venice I can make what merchandise I will. Go,   121
Tubal, and meet me at our synagogue; go, good Tubal;
at our synagogue, Tubal.   *Exeunt.*

❖

3.2   *Enter Bassanio, Portia, Gratiano, [Nerissa,] and
all their trains.*

PORTIA
   I pray you, tarry. Pause a day or two
   Before you hazard, for in choosing wrong   2
   I lose your company. Therefore forbear awhile.
   There's something tells me, but it is not love,
   I would not lose you; and you know yourself,

108 break go bankrupt   **114 Leah** Shylock's wife   **119 fee** hire.   **officer**
bailiff.   **bespeak** engage   **121 make . . . I will** drive whatever bargains I
please

3.2. Location: Belmont. Portia's house.
2 in choosing in your choosing

Hate counsels not in such a quality.   6
But lest you should not understand me well—
And yet a maiden hath no tongue but thought—
I would detain you here some month or two
Before you venture for me. I could teach you
How to choose right, but then I am forsworn.
So will I never be. So may you miss me.   12
But if you do, you'll make me wish a sin,
That I had been forsworn. Beshrew your eyes,
They have o'erlooked me and divided me!   15
One half of me is yours, the other half yours—
Mine own, I would say; but if mine, then yours,
And so all yours. O, these naughty times   18
Puts bars between the owners and their rights!   19
And so, though yours, not yours. Prove it so,   20
Let Fortune go to hell for it, not I.
I speak too long, but 'tis to peise the time,   22
To eke it and to draw it out in length,   23
To stay you from election.

BASSANIO   Let me choose,
For as I am, I live upon the rack.

PORTIA
Upon the rack, Bassanio? Then confess   26
What treason there is mingled with your love.   27

BASSANIO
None but that ugly treason of mistrust,   28
Which makes me fear th' enjoying of my love.   29
There may as well be amity and life
'Tween snow and fire, as treason and my love.

PORTIA
Ay, but I fear you speak upon the rack,
Where men enforcèd do speak anything.

BASSANIO
Promise me life, and I'll confess the truth.

---

6 quality way, manner   **12 So . . . So** that . . . therefore.   **miss**
i.e., fail to win   **15 o'erlooked** bewitched   **18 naughty** worthless, wicked   **19 bars** barriers   **20 Prove it so** if it prove so
22 peise retard (by hanging on of weights)   **23 eke** eke out, augment   **26–27 confess What treason** (The rack was used to force
traitors to confess.)   **28 mistrust** misapprehension   **29 fear** fearful
about

PORTIA
  Well then, confess and live.
BASSANIO   "Confess and love"
  Had been the very sum of my confession.
  O happy torment, when my torturer
  Doth teach me answers for deliverance!
  But let me to my fortune and the caskets.   39
PORTIA
  Away, then! I am locked in one of them.
  If you do love me, you will find me out.
  Nerissa and the rest, stand all aloof.   42
  Let music sound while he doth make his choice;
  Then, if he lose, he makes a swanlike end,   44
  Fading in music. That the comparison
  May stand more proper, my eye shall be the stream
  And watery deathbed for him. He may win;
  And what is music then? Then music is
  Even as the flourish when true subjects bow   49
  To a new-crownèd monarch. Such it is
  As are those dulcet sounds in break of day
  That creep into the dreaming bridegroom's ear
  And summon him to marriage. Now he goes,
  With no less presence, but with much more love,
  Than young Alcides, when he did redeem   55
  The virgin tribute paid by howling Troy   56
  To the sea monster. I stand for sacrifice;   57
  The rest aloof are the Dardanian wives,   58
  With blearèd visages, come forth to view   59
  The issue of th' exploit. Go, Hercules!   60
  Live thou, I live. With much, much more dismay   61
  I view the fight than thou that mak'st the fray.

---

39 fortune . . . caskets (Presumably the curtains are drawn at about
this point, as in the previous "casket" scenes, revealing the three
caskets.)   **42 aloof** apart, at a distance   **44 swanlike** (Swans were
believed to sing when they came to die.)   **49 flourish** sounding of
trumpets   **55 Alcides** (Hercules rescued Hesione, daughter of the Trojan king Laomedon, from a monster to which, by command of Neptune,
she was about to be sacrificed. Hercules was rewarded, however, not
with the lady's love, but with a famous pair of horses.)   **56 howling**
lamenting   **57 stand for sacrifice** represent the sacrificial victim
58 Dardanian Trojan   **59 blearèd** weeping   **60 issue** outcome   **61 Live
thou** if you live

*A song, [sung by one of Portia's train,] the whilst
Bassanio comments on the caskets to himself.*

[*Song.*]

Tell me where is fancy bred,	63
Or in the heart or in the head?	64
How begot, how nourishèd?	
Reply, reply.	
It is engenderèd in the eyes,	67
With gazing fed, and fancy dies	
In the cradle where it lies.	69
Let us all ring fancy's knell.	
I'll begin it—Ding, dong, bell.	

ALL   Ding, dong, bell.

BASSANIO

So may the outward shows be least themselves;	73
The world is still deceived with ornament.	74
In law, what plea so tainted and corrupt	
But, being seasoned with a gracious voice,	
Obscures the show of evil? In religion,	
What damnèd error but some sober brow	
Will bless it and approve it with a text,	79
Hiding the grossness with fair ornament?	
There is no vice so simple but assumes	81
Some mark of virtue on his outward parts.	82
How many cowards, whose hearts are all as false	
As stairs of sand, wear yet upon their chins	84
The beards of Hercules and frowning Mars,	
Who, inward searched, have livers white as milk!	86
And these assume but valor's excrement	87
To render them redoubted. Look on beauty,	88
And you shall see 'tis purchased by the weight,	
Which therein works a miracle in nature,	

63 fancy love   **64 Or** either   **67 eyes** (Love entered the heart especially
through the eyes.)   **69 In the cradle** i.e., in its infancy, in the eyes
73 be least themselves least represent the inner reality   **74 still** ever
79 approve confirm   **81 simple** unadulterated   **82 his** its   **84 stairs**
steps   **86 livers** (The liver was thought to be the seat of courage; for it
to be deserted by the blood would be the condition of cowardice.)
87 excrement outgrowth, such as a beard (as in this case) or finger-
nails   **88 redoubted** feared

Making them lightest that wear most of it.   91
So are those crispèd snaky golden locks,   92
Which maketh such wanton gambols with the wind
Upon supposèd fairness, often known   94
To be the dowry of a second head,   95
The skull that bred them in the sepulcher.   96
Thus ornament is but the guilèd shore   97
To a most dangerous sea, the beauteous scarf
Veiling an Indian beauty; in a word,   99
The seeming truth which cunning times put on
To entrap the wisest. Therefore, thou gaudy gold,
Hard food for Midas, I will none of thee;   102
Nor none of thee, thou pale and common drudge   103
'Tween man and man. But thou, thou meager lead,   104
Which rather threaten'st than dost promise aught,
Thy paleness moves me more than eloquence;
And here choose I. Joy be the consequence!

PORTIA [*Aside*]
How all the other passions fleet to air,
As doubtful thoughts, and rash-embraced despair,   109
And shuddering fear, and green-eyed jealousy!
O love, be moderate, allay thy ecstasy,
In measure rain thy joy, scant this excess!   112
I feel too much thy blessing. Make it less,
For fear I surfeit.

BASSANIO [*Opening the leaden casket*]
                    What find I here?
Fair Portia's counterfeit! What demigod   115
Hath come so near creation? Move these eyes?
Or whether, riding on the balls of mine,
Seem they in motion? Here are severed lips,
Parted with sugar breath; so sweet a bar   119
Should sunder such sweet friends. Here in her hairs   120

91 lightest most lascivious (with pun on the sense of "least heavy")
92 crispèd curly   **94 Upon supposèd fairness** i.e., on a woman supposed
beautiful and fairhaired   **95–96 To . . . sepulcher** i.e., to be a wig of hair
taken from a woman now dead   **97 guilèd** treacherous   **99 Indian** i.e.,
swarthy, not fair   **102 Midas** the Phrygian king whose touch turned
everything to gold, including his food   **103–104 pale . . . man** i.e., silver,
used in commerce   **109 As** such as   **112 rain** rain down, or perhaps
rein. **scant** lessen   **115 counterfeit** portrait. **demigod** i.e., the painter
as creator   **119 so sweet a bar** i.e., Portia's breath   **120 sweet friends**
i.e., her lips

The painter plays the spider, and hath woven
A golden mesh t' entrap the hearts of men
Faster than gnats in cobwebs. But her eyes—   123
How could he see to do them? Having made one,
Methinks it should have power to steal both his
And leave itself unfurnished. Yet look how far   126
The substance of my praise doth wrong this shadow   127
In underprizing it, so far this shadow
Doth limp behind the substance. Here's the scroll,   129
The continent and summary of my fortune.   130
  [*Reads*.] "You that choose not by the view,
          Chance as fair, and choose as true!   132
          Since this fortune falls to you,
          Be content and seek no new.
          If you be well pleased with this,
          And hold your fortune for your bliss,
          Turn you where your lady is
          And claim her with a loving kiss."
A gentle scroll. Fair lady, by your leave,
I come by note, to give and to receive.   140
Like one of two contending in a prize,   141
That thinks he hath done well in people's eyes,
Hearing applause and universal shout,
Giddy in spirit, still gazing in a doubt
Whether those peals of praise be his or no,   145
So, thrice-fair lady, stand I even so,
As doubtful whether what I see be true,
Until confirmed, signed, ratified by you.
PORTIA
You see me, Lord Bassanio, where I stand,
Such as I am. Though for myself alone
I would not be ambitious in my wish
To wish myself much better, yet for you
I would be trebled twenty times myself,
A thousand times more fair, ten thousand times more
  rich,
That only to stand high in your account   155

123 Faster more tightly   **126 unfurnished** i.e., without a companion.
look how far however far   **127 shadow** painting   **129 the substance** the
subject, i.e., Portia   **130 continent** container   **132 Chance as fair** hazard
as fortunately   **140 by note** as indicated (i.e., as directed by the scroll)
141 prize competition   **145 his** for him   **155 account** estimation

I might in virtues, beauties, livings, friends,   156
Exceed account. But the full sum of me   157
Is sum of something, which, to term in gross,   158
Is an unlessoned girl, unschooled, unpracticèd;
Happy in this, she is not yet so old
But she may learn; happier than this,
She is not bred so dull but she can learn;
Happiest of all is that her gentle spirit
Commits itself to yours to be directed,
As from her lord, her governor, her king.
Myself and what is mine to you and yours
Is now converted. But now I was the lord   167
Of this fair mansion, master of my servants,
Queen o'er myself; and even now, but now,
This house, these servants, and this same myself
Are yours, my lord's. I give them with this ring,
Which when you part from, lose, or give away,
Let it presage the ruin of your love
And be my vantage to exclaim on you.   174

        [She puts a ring on his finger.]

BASSANIO
Madam, you have bereft me of all words.
Only my blood speaks to you in my veins,
And there is such confusion in my powers   177
As, after some oration fairly spoke
By a belovèd prince, there doth appear
Among the buzzing pleasèd multitude,
Where every something being blent together   181
Turns to a wild of nothing save of joy   182
Expressed and not expressed. But when this ring   183
Parts from this finger, then parts life from hence.
O, then be bold to say Bassanio's dead!

NERISSA
My lord and lady, it is now our time,
That have stood by and seen our wishes prosper,   187
To cry, good joy. Good joy, my lord and lady!

---

156 livings possessions   **157 account** calculation   **158 something** i.e., at
least something.   **term in gross** relate in full   **167 But now** a moment
ago   **174 exclaim on** reproach   **177 powers** faculties   **181–183 Where
. . . expressed** i.e., in which every individual utterance, being blended
and confused, turns into a hubbub of joy that speaks and yet in no
understood tongue   **187 That** we who

GRATIANO
My lord Bassanio and my gentle lady,
I wish you all the joy that you can wish—
For I am sure you can wish none from me.   191
And when your honors mean to solemnize
The bargain of your faith, I do beseech you,
Even at that time I may be married too.

BASSANIO
With all my heart, so thou canst get a wife.   195

GRATIANO
I thank your lordship, you have got me one.
My eyes, my lord, can look as swift as yours.
You saw the mistress, I beheld the maid;   198
You loved, I loved; for intermission   199
No more pertains to me, my lord, than you.
Your fortune stood upon the caskets there,
And so did mine too, as the matter falls;
For wooing here until I sweat again,   203
And swearing till my very roof was dry   204
With oaths of love, at last, if promise last,   205
I got a promise of this fair one here
To have her love, provided that your fortune
Achieved her mistress.

PORTIA   Is this true, Nerissa?

NERISSA
Madam, it is, so you stand pleased withal.   209

BASSANIO
And do you, Gratiano, mean good faith?

GRATIANO   Yes, faith, my lord.

BASSANIO
Our feast shall be much honored in your marriage.

GRATIANO   We'll play with them the first boy for a thou-   213
sand ducats.

NERISSA   What, and stake down?   215

---

191 For . . . me i.e., I'm sure I can't wish you any more joy than you
could wish for yourselves   195 so provided   198 maid (Nerissa is a
lady-in-waiting, not a house servant.)   199 intermission delay (in loving)   203 sweat again sweated repeatedly   204 roof roof of my mouth
205 if promise last i.e., if Nerissa's promise should last, hold out
209 so provided   213 play wager   215 stake down cash placed in
advance. (But Gratiano, in his reply, turns the phrase into a bawdy joke;
stake down to him suggests a nonerect phallus.)

GRATIANO No, we shall ne'er win at that sport, and
stake down.
But who comes here? Lorenzo and his infidel?
What, and my old Venetian friend Salerio?

*Enter Lorenzo, Jessica, and Salerio, a messenger
from Venice.*

BASSANIO
Lorenzo and Salerio, welcome hither,
If that the youth of my new interest here   221
Have power to bid you welcome.—By your leave,
I bid my very friends and countrymen,   223
Sweet Portia, welcome.
PORTIA   So do I, my lord.
They are entirely welcome.
LORENZO
I thank your honor. For my part, my lord,
My purpose was not to have seen you here,
But meeting with Salerio by the way,
He did intreat me, past all saying nay,
To come with him along.
SALERIO   I did, my lord,
And I have reason for it. Signor Antonio
Commends him to you. [*He gives Bassanio a letter.*]
BASSANIO   Ere I ope his letter,   232
I pray you tell me how my good friend doth.
SALERIO
Not sick, my lord, unless it be in mind,
Nor well, unless in mind. His letter there
Will show you his estate. [*Bassanio*] open[*s*] *the letter.* 236
GRATIANO
Nerissa, cheer yond stranger, bid her welcome.   237
Your hand, Salerio. What's the news from Venice?
How doth that royal merchant, good Antonio?   239
I know he will be glad of our success;
We are the Jasons, we have won the fleece.   241

---

221 youth . . . interest i.e., newness of my household authority
223 very true **232 Commends him** desires to be remembered **236 estate** condition **237 stranger** i.e., Jessica **239 royal merchant** i.e., chief
among merchants **241 Jasons . . . fleece** (Cf. 1.1.170–172.)

SALERIO
   I would you had won the fleece that he hath lost.

PORTIA
   There are some shrewd contents in yond same paper   243
   That steals the color from Bassanio's cheek—
   Some dear friend dead, else nothing in the world
   Could turn so much the constitution
   Of any constant man. What, worse and worse?   247
   With leave, Bassanio; I am half yourself,
   And I must freely have the half of anything
   That this same paper brings you.

BASSANIO   O sweet Portia,
   Here are a few of the unpleasant'st words
   That ever blotted paper! Gentle lady,
   When I did first impart my love to you,
   I freely told you all the wealth I had
   Ran in my veins, I was a gentleman;
   And then I told you true. And yet, dear lady,
   Rating myself at nothing, you shall see
   How much I was a braggart. When I told you
   My state was nothing, I should then have told you   259
   That I was worse than nothing; for indeed
   I have engaged myself to a dear friend,
   Engaged my friend to his mere enemy,   262
   To feed my means. Here is a letter, lady,
   The paper as the body of my friend,
   And every word in it a gaping wound
   Issuing lifeblood. But is it true, Salerio?
   Hath all his ventures failed? What, not one hit?   267
   From Tripolis, from Mexico, and England,
   From Lisbon, Barbary, and India,
   And not one vessel scape the dreadful touch
   Of merchant-marring rocks?

SALERIO   Not one, my lord.   271
   Besides, it should appear that if he had
   The present money to discharge the Jew,   273
   He would not take it. Never did I know   274
   A creature that did bear the shape of man

---

243 shrewd cursed, grievous   **247 constant** settled, not swayed by
passion   **259 state** estate   **262 mere** absolute   **267 hit** success
271 merchant merchant ship   **273 present** available.   **discharge** pay
off   **274 He** i.e., Shylock

So keen and greedy to confound a man.   276
He plies the Duke at morning and at night,
And doth impeach the freedom of the state   278
If they deny him justice. Twenty merchants,
The Duke himself, and the magnificoes   280
Of greatest port have all persuaded with him,   281
But none can drive him from the envious plea
Of forfeiture, of justice, and his bond.

JESSICA

When I was with him I have heard him swear
To Tubal and to Chus, his countrymen,
That he would rather have Antonio's flesh
Than twenty times the value of the sum
That he did owe him; and I know, my lord,
If law, authority, and power deny not,
It will go hard with poor Antonio.

PORTIA

Is it your dear friend that is thus in trouble?

BASSANIO

The dearest friend to me, the kindest man,
The best-conditioned and unwearied spirit   293
In doing courtesies, and one in whom
The ancient Roman honor more appears
Than any that draws breath in Italy.

PORTIA   What sum owes he the Jew?

BASSANIO

For me, three thousand ducats.

PORTIA   What, no more?
Pay him six thousand, and deface the bond;   299
Double six thousand, and then treble that,
Before a friend of this description
Shall lose a hair through Bassanio's fault.
First go with me to church and call me wife,
And then away to Venice to your friend;
For never shall you lie by Portia's side
With an unquiet soul. You shall have gold
To pay the petty debt twenty times over.
When it is paid, bring your true friend along.

---

276 keen cruel.   **confound** destroy   **278 impeach . . . state** i.e., call in question the ability of Venice to defend legally the freedom of commerce of its
citizens   **280 magnificoes** chief men of Venice   **281 port** dignity.   **persuaded**
argued   **293 best-conditioned** best natured   **299 deface** erase

My maid Nerissa and myself meantime
Will live as maids and widows. Come, away!
For you shall hence upon your wedding day.
Bid your friends welcome, show a merry cheer;   312
Since you are dear bought, I will love you dear.
But let me hear the letter of your friend.

BASSANIO [*Reads*] "Sweet Bassanio, my ships have all
miscarried, my creditors grow cruel, my estate is very
low, my bond to the Jew is forfeit; and since in paying
it, it is impossible I should live, all debts are cleared
between you and I, if I might but see you at my death.
Notwithstanding, use your pleasure; if your love do
not persuade you to come, let not my letter."

PORTIA
O love, dispatch all business, and begone!

BASSANIO
Since I have your good leave to go away,
I will make haste; but till I come again,
No bed shall e'er be guilty of my stay,
Nor rest be interposer twixt us twain.   *Exeunt.*

✤

3.3   *Enter [Shylock] the Jew and Solanio and
Antonio and the Jailer.*

SHYLOCK
Jailer, look to him. Tell not me of mercy.
This is the fool that lent out money gratis.
Jailer, look to him.

ANTONIO   Hear me yet, good Shylock.

SHYLOCK
I'll have my bond. Speak not against my bond!
I have sworn an oath that I will have my bond.
Thou calledst me dog before thou hadst a cause,
But since I am a dog, beware my fangs.
The Duke shall grant me justice. I do wonder,
Thou naughty jailer, that thou art so fond   9

312 cheer countenance

3.3. Location: Venice. A street.
9 naughty worthless. **fond** foolish

To come abroad with him at his request.   10
ANTONIO   I pray thee, hear me speak.
SHYLOCK
  I'll have my bond. I will not hear thee speak.
  I'll have my bond, and therefore speak no more.
  I'll not be made a soft and dull-eyed fool,
  To shake the head, relent, and sigh, and yield
  To Christian intercessors. Follow not;
  I'll have no speaking. I will have my bond.   *Exit Jew.*
SOLANIO
  It is the most impenetrable cur
  That ever kept with men.
ANTONIO   Let him alone.   19
  I'll follow him no more with bootless prayers.   20
  He seeks my life. His reason well I know:
  I oft delivered from his forfeitures
  Many that have at times made moan to me;
  Therefore he hates me.
SOLANIO   I am sure the Duke
  Will never grant this forfeiture to hold.
ANTONIO
  The Duke cannot deny the course of law;
  For the commodity that strangers have   27
  With us in Venice, if it be denied,
  Will much impeach the justice of the state,
  Since that the trade and profit of the city   30
  Consisteth of all nations. Therefore go.
  These griefs and losses have so bated me   32
  That I shall hardly spare a pound of flesh
  Tomorrow to my bloody creditor.
  Well, jailer, on. Pray God Bassanio come
  To see me pay his debt, and then I care not.   *Exeunt.*

❖

3.4   *Enter Portia, Nerissa, Lorenzo, Jessica, and
          [Balthasar,] a man of Portia's.*

10 abroad outside   **19 kept** associated, dwelt   **20 bootless** unavailing
27 commodity facilities or privileges for trading.   **strangers** nonciti-
zens, including Jews   **30 Since that** since   **32 bated** reduced

3.4. Location: Belmont. Portia's house.

LORENZO
    Madam, although I speak it in your presence,
    You have a noble and a true conceit   2
    Of godlike amity, which appears most strongly
    In bearing thus the absence of your lord.
    But if you knew to whom you show this honor,
    How true a gentleman you send relief,
    How dear a lover of my lord your husband,
    I know you would be prouder of the work
    Than customary bounty can enforce you.   9

PORTIA
    I never did repent for doing good,
    Nor shall not now; for in companions
    That do converse and waste the time together,   12
    Whose souls do bear an equal yoke of love,
    There must be needs a like proportion   14
    Of lineaments, of manners, and of spirit;   15
    Which makes me think that this Antonio,
    Being the bosom lover of my lord,
    Must needs be like my lord. If it be so,
    How little is the cost I have bestowed
    In purchasing the semblance of my soul   20
    From out the state of hellish cruelty!
    This comes too near the praising of myself;
    Therefore no more of it. Hear other things:
    Lorenzo, I commit into your hands
    The husbandry and manage of my house   25
    Until my lord's return. For mine own part,
    I have toward heaven breathed a secret vow
    To live in prayer and contemplation,
    Only attended by Nerissa here,
    Until her husband and my lord's return.
    There is a monastery two miles off,
    And there we will abide. I do desire you
    Not to deny this imposition,   33
    The which my love and some necessity
    Now lays upon you.

---

2 conceit understanding   **9 Than . . . you** than ordinary benevolence
can make you   **12 waste** spend   **14 must be needs** must be   **15 line-
aments** physical features   **20 the semblance of my soul** i.e., Antonio, so
like my Bassanio   **25 husbandry and manage** care of the household
33 deny this imposition refuse this charge imposed

LORENZO   Madam, with all my heart.
I shall obey you in all fair commands.
PORTIA
My people do already know my mind,
And will acknowledge you and Jessica
In place of Lord Bassanio and myself.
So fare you well till we shall meet again.
LORENZO
Fair thoughts and happy hours attend on you!
JESSICA
I wish your ladyship all heart's content.
PORTIA
I thank you for your wish and am well pleased
To wish it back on you. Fare you well, Jessica.
                    Exeunt [Jessica and Lorenzo].
Now, Balthasar,
As I have ever found thee honest-true,
So let me find thee still. Take this same letter,
                    [*Giving a letter*]
And use thou all th' endeavor of a man
In speed to Padua. See thou render this
Into my cousin's hands, Doctor Bellario;
And look what notes and garments he doth give thee,   51
Bring them, I pray thee, with imagined speed   52
Unto the traject, to the common ferry   53
Which trades to Venice. Waste no time in words,   54
But get thee gone. I shall be there before thee.
BALTHASAR
Madam, I go with all convenient speed.   [*Exit.*] 56
PORTIA
Come on, Nerissa, I have work in hand
That you yet know not of. We'll see our husbands
Before they think of us.
NERISSA   Shall they see us?
PORTIA
They shall, Nerissa, but in such a habit   60
That they shall think we are accomplishèd   61

---

51 look what whatever   **52 imagined** imaginable   **53 traject** ferry.
(Italian *traghetto*.)   **54 trades** plies back and forth   **56 convenient** due,
proper   **60 habit** apparel, garb   **61 accomplishèd** supplied

With that we lack. I'll hold thee any wager,   62
When we are both accoutred like young men,
I'll prove the prettier fellow of the two,
And wear my dagger with the braver grace,
And speak between the change of man and boy
With a reed voice, and turn two mincing steps
Into a manly stride, and speak of frays
Like a fine bragging youth, and tell quaint lies,   69
How honorable ladies sought my love,
Which I denying, they fell sick and died—
I could not do withal! Then I'll repent,   72
And wish, for all that, that I had not killed them;
And twenty of these puny lies I'll tell,   74
That men shall swear I have discontinued school   75
Above a twelvemonth. I have within my mind   76
A thousand raw tricks of these bragging Jacks,   77
Which I will practice.
NERISSA   Why, shall we turn to men?   78
PORTIA   Fie, what a question's that,
If thou wert near a lewd interpreter!
But come, I'll tell thee all my whole device
When I am in my coach, which stays for us
At the park gate; and therefore haste away,
For we must measure twenty miles today.   *Exeunt.*

❧

3.5   *Enter [Launcelot the] Clown and Jessica.*

LAUNCELOT   Yes truly, for look you, the sins of the father are to be laid upon the children; therefore, I promise you, I fear you. I was always plain with you, and   3
so now I speak my agitation of the matter. Therefore   4
be o' good cheer, for truly I think you are damned.

---

62 that that which (with a bawdy suggestion)   **69 quaint** elaborate,
clever   **72 do withal** help it   **74 puny** childish   **75–76 I . . . twelvemonth** i.e., that I am no mere schoolboy   **76 Above** more than
77 Jacks fellows   **78 turn to** turn into. (But Portia sees the occasion
for a bawdy quibble on the idea of "turning toward, lying next to.")

3.5. Location: Belmont. Outside Portia's house.
3 fear you fear for you   **4 agitation** consideration

There is but one hope in it that can do you any good,
and that is but a kind of bastard hope neither.   7
JESSICA   And what hope is that, I pray thee?
LAUNCELOT   Marry, you may partly hope that your father got you not, that you are not the Jew's daughter.   10
JESSICA   That were a kind of bastard hope indeed! So
the sins of my mother should be visited upon me.
LAUNCELOT   Truly then I fear you are damned both by
father and mother. Thus when I shun Scylla, your fa-   14
ther, I fall into Charybdis, your mother. Well, you are   15
gone both ways.   16
JESSICA   I shall be saved by my husband. He hath made   17
me a Christian.
LAUNCELOT   Truly, the more to blame he! We were
Christians enough before, e'en as many as could well   20
live one by another. This making of Christians will   21
raise the price of hogs. If we grow all to be pork eaters,
we shall not shortly have a rasher on the coals for   23
money.   24

   Enter Lorenzo.

JESSICA   I'll tell my husband, Launcelot, what you say.
Here he comes.
LORENZO   I shall grow jealous of you shortly, Launcelot,
if you thus get my wife into corners.
JESSICA   Nay, you need not fear us, Lorenzo. Launcelot
and I are out. He tells me flatly there's no mercy for me   30
in heaven because I am a Jew's daughter; and he says
you are no good member of the commonwealth, for in
converting Jews to Christians you raise the price of
pork.
LORENZO   I shall answer that better to the commonwealth than you can the getting up of the Negro's
belly. The Moor is with child by you, Launcelot.

---

7 neither i.e., to be sure   **10 got** begot   **14, 15 Scylla, Charybdis** twin
dangers of the *Odyssey*, 12.255, a monster and a whirlpool guarding the
straits presumably between Italy and Sicily   **16 gone** done for   **17 I . . .
husband** (Cf. 1 Corinthians 7:14: "the unbelieving wife is sanctified by
the husband.")   **20 enough** i.e., there were enough of us   **21 one by
another** together   **23 rasher** i.e., of bacon   **23–24 for money** even for
ready money, at any price   **30 are out** have fallen out

LAUNCELOT It is much that the Moor should be more 38
 than reason; but if she be less than an honest woman, 39
 she is indeed more than I took her for.

LORENZO How every fool can play upon the word! I
 think the best grace of wit will shortly turn into si- 42
 lence, and discourse grow commendable in none only
 but parrots. Go in, sirrah, bid them prepare for
 dinner.

LAUNCELOT That is done, sir. They have all stomachs. 46

LORENZO Goodly Lord, what a wit-snapper are you!
 Then bid them prepare dinner.

LAUNCELOT That is done too, sir, only "cover" is the 49
 word.

LORENZO Will you cover then, sir? 51

LAUNCELOT Not so, sir, neither. I know my duty.

LORENZO Yet more quarreling with occasion! Wilt thou 53
 show the whole wealth of thy wit in an instant? I pray
 thee, understand a plain man in his plain meaning: go
 to thy fellows, bid them cover the table, serve in the
 meat, and we will come in to dinner. 57

LAUNCELOT For the table, sir, it shall be served in; for 58
 the meat, sir, it shall be covered; for your coming in to 59
 dinner, sir, why, let it be as humors and conceits shall 60
 govern.   *Exit Clown.*

LORENZO

 O dear discretion, how his words are suited! 62
 The fool hath planted in his memory
 An army of good words; and I do know
 A many fools, that stand in better place, 65
 Garnished like him, that for a tricksy word 66
 Defy the matter. How cheer'st thou, Jessica? 67

38–39 more than reason larger than is reasonable (with wordplay on
Moor, more, continued in l. 40) **39 honest** chaste **42 best grace** high-
est quality **46 stomachs** appetites **49, 51 cover** spread the table for
the meal. (But in his next speech Launcelot uses the word to mean "put
on one's hat.") **53 Yet . . . occasion** i.e., still quibbling at every opportunity **57 meat** food **58 table** (Here Launcelot quibblingly uses the word
to mean the food itself.) **59 covered** (Here used in the sense of providing a cover for each separate dish.) **60 humors and conceits** whims and
fancies **62 discretion** discrimination. **suited** suited to the occasion
65 A many many. **better place** higher social station **66 Garnished** i.e.,
furnished with words. **tricksy** playful **66–67 that . . . matter** who for
the sake of ingenious wordplay do violence to common sense **67 How
cheer'st thou** i.e., what cheer

And now, good sweet, say thy opinion,
How dost thou like the Lord Bassanio's wife?

JESSICA
Past all expressing. It is very meet   70
The Lord Bassanio live an upright life,
For, having such a blessing in his lady,
He finds the joys of heaven here on earth;
And if on earth he do not merit it,
In reason he should never come to heaven.   75
Why, if two gods should play some heavenly match
And on the wager lay two earthly women,   77
And Portia one, there must be something else   78
Pawned with the other, for the poor rude world   79
Hath not her fellow.

LORENZO   Even such a husband
Hast thou of me as she is for a wife.

JESSICA
Nay, but ask my opinion too of that!

LORENZO
I will anon. First let us go to dinner.

JESSICA
Nay, let me praise you while I have a stomach.   84

LORENZO
No, pray thee, let it serve for table talk;
Then, howsoe'er thou speak'st, 'mong other things
I shall digest it.

JESSICA   Well, I'll set you forth.   *Exeunt.*   87

❧

---

70 meet fitting   **75 In reason** it stands to reason. (Jessica jokes that for Bassanio to receive unmerited bliss on earth—unmerited because no person can earn bliss through his or her own deserving—is to run the risk of eternal damnation.)   **77 lay** stake   **78 else** more   **79 Pawned** staked, wagered   **84 stomach** (1) appetite (2) inclination   **87 digest** (1) ponder, analyze (2) "swallow," put up with (with a play also on the gastronomic sense).   **set you forth** (1) serve you up, as at a feast (2) set forth your praises

4.1 *Enter the Duke, the Magnificoes, Antonio,*
Bassanio, [Salerio,] and Gratiano [with others.
The judges take their places.]

DUKE What, is Antonio here?

ANTONIO Ready, so please Your Grace.

DUKE

I am sorry for thee. Thou art come to answer   3
A stony adversary, an inhuman wretch
Uncapable of pity, void and empty
From any dram of mercy.

ANTONIO   I have heard   6
Your Grace hath ta'en great pains to qualify   7
His rigorous course; but since he stands obdurate
And that no lawful means can carry me
Out of his envy's reach, I do oppose   10
My patience to his fury and am armed
To suffer with a quietness of spirit
The very tyranny and rage of his.   13

DUKE

Go one, and call the Jew into the court.

SALERIO

He is ready at the door; he comes, my lord.

Enter Shylock.

DUKE

Make room, and let him stand before our face.   16
Shylock, the world thinks, and I think so too,
That thou but leadest this fashion of thy malice   18
To the last hour of act, and then 'tis thought   19
Thou'lt show thy mercy and remorse more strange   20
Than is thy strange apparent cruelty;   21
And where thou now exacts the penalty,
Which is a pound of this poor merchant's flesh,

4.1. Location: Venice. A court of justice. Benches, etc., are provided for
the justices.
3 answer defend yourself against. (A legal term.) **6 dram** 60 grains
apothecaries' weight, a tiny quantity **7 qualify** moderate **10 envy's**
malice's **13 tyranny** cruelty **16 our** (The royal plural.) **18 thou . . .**
fashion you only maintain this pretense or form **19 act** action, performance **20 remorse** pity. **strange** remarkable **21 apparent** conspicu-
ous, overt

Thou wilt not only loose the forfeiture,   24
But, touched with human gentleness and love,
Forgive a moiety of the principal,   26
Glancing an eye of pity on his losses
That have of late so huddled on his back—
Enough to press a royal merchant down
And pluck commiseration of his state
From brassy bosoms and rough hearts of flint,   31
From stubborn Turks and Tartars never trained
To offices of tender courtesy.
We all expect a gentle answer, Jew.

SHYLOCK

I have possessed Your Grace of what I purpose,   35
And by our holy Sabbath have I sworn
To have the due and forfeit of my bond.
If you deny it, let the danger light   38
Upon your charter and your city's freedom!   39
You'll ask me why I rather choose to have
A weight of carrion flesh than to receive
Three thousand ducats. I'll not answer that,
But say it is my humor. Is it answered?   43
What if my house be troubled with a rat
And I be pleased to give ten thousand ducats
To have it baned? What, are you answered yet?   46
Some men there are love not a gaping pig,   47
Some that are mad if they behold a cat,
And others, when the bagpipe sings i' the nose,
Cannot contain their urine; for affection,   50
Mistress of passion, sways it to the mood
Of what it likes or loathes. Now, for your answer:
As there is no firm reason to be rendered
Why he cannot abide a gaping pig,   54
Why he a harmless necessary cat,   55
Why he a woolen bagpipe, but of force   56
Must yield to such inevitable shame

---

24 loose release, waive   **26 moiety** part, portion   **31 brassy** unfeeling,
i.e., hard like brass   **35 possessed** informed   **38 danger** injury
39 Upon . . . freedom (See 3.2.278.)   **43 humor** whim   **46 baned** killed,
especially by poison or ratsbane   **47 love** who love.   **gaping pig** pig
roasted whole with its mouth open   **50 affection** feeling, inclination
54, 55, 56 he, he, he one person, another, yet another   **56 woolen** i.e.,
with flannel-covered bag

As to offend, himself being offended;
So can I give no reason, nor I will not,
More than a lodged hate and a certain loathing   60
I bear Antonio, that I follow thus
A losing suit against him. Are you answered?   62

BASSANIO
This is no answer, thou unfeeling man,
To excuse the current of thy cruelty.   64

SHYLOCK
I am not bound to please thee with my answers.

BASSANIO
Do all men kill the things they do not love?

SHYLOCK
Hates any man the thing he would not kill?

BASSANIO
Every offense is not a hate at first.

SHYLOCK
What, wouldst thou have a serpent sting thee twice?

ANTONIO
I pray you, think you question with the Jew.   70
You may as well go stand upon the beach
And bid the main flood bate his usual height;   72
You may as well use question with the wolf   73
Why he hath made the ewe bleat for the lamb;
You may as well forbid the mountain pines
To wag their high tops and to make no noise
When they are fretten with the gusts of heaven;   77
You may as well do anything most hard
As seek to soften that—than which what's harder?—
His Jewish heart. Therefore I do beseech you
Make no more offers, use no farther means,
But with all brief and plain conveniency   82
Let me have judgment, and the Jew his will.

BASSANIO
For thy three thousand ducats here is six.

SHYLOCK
If every ducat in six thousand ducats

60 lodged settled, steadfast.   **certain** unwavering, fixed   **62 losing**
unprofitable   **64 current** flow, tendency   **70 think** bear in mind.
question argue   **72 main flood** sea at high tide.   **bate** abate   **73 use**
question with interrogate   **77 fretten** fretted, i.e., disturbed, ruffled
82 conveniency propriety

Were in six parts, and every part a ducat,
I would not draw them. I would have my bond. 87

DUKE
How shalt thou hope for mercy, rendering none?

SHYLOCK
What judgment shall I dread, doing no wrong?
You have among you many a purchased slave,
Which, like your asses and your dogs and mules,
You use in abject and in slavish parts, 92
Because you bought them. Shall I say to you,
"Let them be free, marry them to your heirs!
Why sweat they under burdens? Let their beds
Be made as soft as yours, and let their palates
Be seasoned with such viands"? You will answer, 97
"The slaves are ours." So do I answer you:
The pound of flesh which I demand of him
Is dearly bought, is mine, and I will have it.
If you deny me, fie upon your law!
There is no force in the decrees of Venice.
I stand for judgment. Answer: shall I have it?

DUKE
Upon my power I may dismiss this court, 104
Unless Bellario, a learnèd doctor,
Whom I have sent for to determine this,
Come here today.

SALERIO   My lord, here stays without 107
A messenger with letters from the doctor,
New come from Padua.

DUKE
Bring us the letters. Call the messenger.

BASSANIO
Good cheer, Antonio! What, man, courage yet!
The Jew shall have my flesh, blood, bones, and all,
Ere thou shalt lose for me one drop of blood.

ANTONIO
I am a tainted wether of the flock, 114
Meetest for death. The weakest kind of fruit 115
Drops earliest to the ground, and so let me.

---

87 draw receive   **92 parts** duties, capacities   **97 viands** food   **104 Upon**
in accordance with   **107 stays without** waits outside   **114 tainted**
wether old and diseased ram   **115 Meetest** fittest

You cannot better be employed, Bassanio,
Than to live still and write mine epitaph.

Enter Nerissa [dressed like a lawyer's clerk].

DUKE
Came you from Padua, from Bellario?
NERISSA
From both, my lord. Bellario greets Your Grace.
                    [*She presents a letter. Shylock whets his knife
                                                    on his shoe.*]
BASSANIO
Why dost thou whet thy knife so earnestly?
SHYLOCK
To cut the forfeiture from that bankrupt there.
GRATIANO
Not on thy sole, but on thy soul, harsh Jew,
Thou mak'st thy knife keen; but no metal can,
No, not the hangman's ax, bear half the keenness   125
Of thy sharp envy. Can no prayers pierce thee?   126
SHYLOCK
No, none that thou hast wit enough to make.
GRATIANO
O, be thou damned, inexecrable dog!   128
And for thy life let justice be accused.   129
Thou almost mak'st me waver in my faith
To hold opinion with Pythagoras,   131
That souls of animals infuse themselves
Into the trunks of men. Thy currish spirit
Governed a wolf who, hanged for human slaughter,   134
Even from the gallows did his fell soul fleet,   135
And, whilst thou layest in thy unhallowed dam,   136
Infused itself in thee; for thy desires
Are wolvish, bloody, starved, and ravenous.

125 hangman's executioner's.   **keenness** (1) sharpness (2) savagery
126 envy malice   **128 inexecrable** that cannot be overly execrated or
detested   **129 for thy life** i.e., because you are allowed to live
131 Pythagoras ancient Greek philosopher who argued for the transmi-
gration of souls   **134 hanged for human slaughter** (A possible allusion
to the ancient practice of trying and punishing animals for various
crimes.)   **135 fell** fierce, cruel.   **fleet** flit, i.e., pass from the body
136 dam mother (usually used of animals)

SHYLOCK

Till thou canst rail the seal from off my bond,   139
Thou but offend'st thy lungs to speak so loud.   140
Repair thy wit, good youth, or it will fall
To cureless ruin. I stand here for law.   142

DUKE

This letter from Bellario doth commend
A young and learnèd doctor to our court.
Where is he?

NERISSA   He attendeth here hard by
To know your answer, whether you'll admit him.

DUKE

With all my heart. Some three or four of you
Go give him courteous conduct to this place.

                      [Exeunt some.]

Meantime the court shall hear Bellario's letter.

  [Reads.] "Your Grace shall understand that at the   150
receipt of your letter I am very sick; but in the instant
that your messenger came, in loving visitation was
with me a young doctor of Rome. His name is Balthasar. I acquainted him with the cause in controversy
between the Jew and Antonio the merchant. We
turned o'er many books together. He is furnished with
my opinion, which, bettered with his own learning,
the greatness whereof I cannot enough commend,
comes with him, at my importunity, to fill up Your   159
Grace's request in my stead. I beseech you, let his lack
of years be no impediment to let him lack a reverend   161
estimation, for I never knew so young a body with so
old a head. I leave him to your gracious acceptance,
whose trial shall better publish his commendation."   164

   Enter Portia for Balthasar [dressed like a doctor
   of laws, escorted].

You hear the learned Bellario, what he writes;

139 rail revile, use abusive language   **140 offend'st** injurest   **142 cureless** incurable   **150 [Reads.]** (In many modern editions, the reading of
the letter is assigned to a clerk, but the original text gives no such indication.)   **159 comes with him** i.e., my opinion is brought by him.   **importunity** insistence   **161 to let him lack** such as would deprive him of   **164 trial**
testing, performance.   **publish** make known   **s.d., for** i.e., disguised as

And here, I take it, is the doctor come.
Give me your hand. Come you from old Bellario?
PORTIA
I did, my lord.
DUKE   You are welcome. Take your place.
                    [*Portia takes her place.*]
Are you acquainted with the difference   169
That holds this present question in the court?
PORTIA
I am informèd throughly of the cause.   171
Which is the merchant here, and which the Jew?
DUKE
Antonio and old Shylock, both stand forth.
PORTIA
Is your name Shylock?
SHYLOCK   Shylock is my name.
PORTIA
Of a strange nature is the suit you follow,
Yet in such rule that the Venetian law   176
Cannot impugn you as you do proceed.—   177
You stand within his danger, do you not?   178
ANTONIO
Ay, so he says.
PORTIA   Do you confess the bond?
ANTONIO
I do.
PORTIA Then must the Jew be merciful.
SHYLOCK
On what compulsion must I? Tell me that.
PORTIA
The quality of mercy is not strained.   182
It droppeth as the gentle rain from heaven
Upon the place beneath. It is twice blest: 184
It blesseth him that gives and him that takes.
'Tis mightiest in the mightiest; it becomes
The thronèd monarch better than his crown.
His scepter shows the force of temporal power,

169 difference argument **171 throughly** thoroughly. **cause** case
176 rule order **177 impugn** find fault with **178 danger** power to do
harm **182 strained** forced, constrained **184 is twice blest** grants a
double blessing

The attribute to awe and majesty,   189
Wherein doth sit the dread and fear of kings.
But mercy is above this sceptered sway;
It is enthronèd in the hearts of kings;
It is an attribute to God himself;
And earthly power doth then show likest God's
When mercy seasons justice. Therefore, Jew,
Though justice be thy plea, consider this,
That in the course of justice none of us
Should see salvation. We do pray for mercy,
And that same prayer doth teach us all to render
The deeds of mercy. I have spoke thus much
To mitigate the justice of thy plea,   201
Which if thou follow, this strict court of Venice
Must needs give sentence 'gainst the merchant there.

SHYLOCK
My deeds upon my head! I crave the law,   204
The penalty and forfeit of my bond.

PORTIA
Is he not able to discharge the money?

BASSANIO
Yes, here I tender it for him in the court,
Yea, twice the sum. If that will not suffice,
I will be bound to pay it ten times o'er,
On forfeit of my hands, my head, my heart.
If this will not suffice, it must appear
That malice bears down truth. And I beseech you,   212
Wrest once the law to your authority.   213
To do a great right, do a little wrong,
And curb this cruel devil of his will.

PORTIA
It must not be. There is no power in Venice
Can alter a decree establishèd.
'Twill be recorded for a precedent,
And many an error by the same example
Will rush into the state. It cannot be.

---

189 attribute to symbol of   **201 To . . . plea** i.e., to moderate your plea
for strict justice   **204 My . . . head** i.e., I am prepared to be judged,
as well as live, by a code of strict justice   **212 bears down truth** over-
whelms righteousness   **213 Wrest once** for once, forcibly subject

SHYLOCK
 A Daniel come to judgment! Yea, a Daniel!   221
 O wise young judge, how I do honor thee!

PORTIA
 I pray you, let me look upon the bond.

SHYLOCK [*Giving the bond*]
 Here 'tis, most reverend doctor, here it is.

PORTIA
 Shylock, there's thrice thy money offered thee.

SHYLOCK
 An oath, an oath, I have an oath in heaven!
 Shall I lay perjury upon my soul?
 No, not for Venice.   Why, this bond is forfeit,

PORTIA
 And lawfully by this the Jew may claim
 A pound of flesh, to be by him cut off
 Nearest the merchant's heart. Be merciful.
 Take thrice thy money; bid me tear the bond.

SHYLOCK
 When it is paid according to the tenor.   233
 It doth appear you are a worthy judge;
 You know the law, your exposition
 Hath been most sound. I charge you by the law,
 Whereof you are a well-deserving pillar,
 Proceed to judgment. By my soul I swear
 There is no power in the tongue of man
 To alter me. I stay here on my bond.   240

ANTONIO
 Most heartily I do beseech the court
 To give the judgment.   Why then, thus it is:

PORTIA
 You must prepare your bosom for his knife.

SHYLOCK
 O noble judge! O excellent young man!

PORTIA
 For the intent and purpose of the law
 Hath full relation to the penalty   246
 Which here appeareth due upon the bond.

221 Daniel (In the apocryphal Book of Susannah, Daniel is the young
judge who rescues Susannah from her false accusers.) **233 tenor**
conditions **240 stay here on** remain committed to, insist upon
246 Hath . . . to is fully in accord with

SHYLOCK
  'Tis very true. O wise and upright judge!
  How much more elder art thou than thy looks!
PORTIA
  Therefore lay bare your bosom.
SHYLOCK   Ay, his breast;
  So says the bond, doth it not, noble judge?
  "Nearest his heart," those are the very words.
PORTIA
  It is so. Are there balance here   253
  To weigh the flesh?
SHYLOCK   I have them ready.
PORTIA
  Have by some surgeon, Shylock, on your charge,   255
  To stop his wounds, lest he do bleed to death.
SHYLOCK
  Is it so nominated in the bond?
PORTIA
  It is not so expressed, but what of that?
  'Twere good you do so much for charity.
SHYLOCK
  I cannot find it; 'tis not in the bond.
PORTIA
  You, merchant, have you anything to say?
ANTONIO
  But little. I am armed and well prepared.   262
  Give me your hand, Bassanio; fare you well!
  Grieve not that I am fall'n to this for you,
  For herein Fortune shows herself more kind
  Than is her custom. It is still her use   266
  To let the wretched man outlive his wealth,
  To view with hollow eye and wrinkled brow
  An age of poverty; from which lingering penance
  Of such misery doth she cut me off.
  Commend me to your honorable wife.
  Tell her the process of Antonio's end.   272
  Say how I loved you, speak me fair in death;   273
  And, when the tale is told, bid her be judge
  Whether Bassanio had not once a love.   275

---

253 balance scales **255 on your charge** at your personal expense **262 armed**
ready **266 still her use** i.e., commonly Fortune's practice **272 process**
story **273 speak me fair** speak well of me **275 a love** a friend's love

Repent but you that you shall lose your friend,   276
And he repents not that he pays your debt.
For if the Jew do cut but deep enough,
I'll pay it instantly with all my heart.

BASSANIO
Antonio, I am married to a wife
Which is as dear to me as life itself;
But life itself, my wife, and all the world
Are not with me esteemed above thy life.
I would lose all, ay, sacrifice them all
Here to this devil, to deliver you.

PORTIA
Your wife would give you little thanks for that,
If she were by to hear you make the offer.   287

GRATIANO
I have a wife who I protest I love;
I would she were in heaven, so she could
Entreat some power to change this currish Jew.

NERISSA
'Tis well you offer it behind her back;
The wish would make else an unquiet house.

SHYLOCK
These be the Christian husbands. I have a daughter;
Would any of the stock of Barabbas   294
Had been her husband rather than a Christian!—
We trifle time. I pray thee, pursue sentence.   296

PORTIA
A pound of that same merchant's flesh is thine.
The court awards it, and the law doth give it.

SHYLOCK   Most rightful judge!

PORTIA
And you must cut this flesh from off his breast.
The law allows it, and the court awards it.

SHYLOCK
Most learnèd judge! A sentence! Come, prepare.

PORTIA
Tarry a little; there is something else.

---

276 Repent but you grieve only   **287 by** nearby   **294 Barabbas** a thief
whom Pontius Pilate set free instead of Christ in response to the people's demand (see Mark 15); also, the villainous protagonist of
Marlowe's *The Jew of Malta*   **296 trifle** waste.   **pursue** proceed with

This bond doth give thee here no jot of blood;
The words expressly are "a pound of flesh."
Take then thy bond, take thou thy pound of flesh;
But in the cutting it if thou dost shed
One drop of Christian blood, thy lands and goods
Are by the laws of Venice confiscate
Unto the state of Venice.

GRATIANO
O upright judge! Mark, Jew. O learnèd judge!

SHYLOCK
Is that the law?

PORTIA   Thyself shalt see the act;
For, as thou urgest justice, be assured
Thou shalt have justice, more than thou desir'st.

GRATIANO
O learnèd judge! Mark, Jew, a learnèd judge!

SHYLOCK
I take this offer, then. Pay the bond thrice
And let the Christian go.

BASSANIO   Here is the money.

PORTIA   Soft!   318
The Jew shall have all justice. Soft, no haste.   319
He shall have nothing but the penalty.

GRATIANO
O Jew! An upright judge, a learnèd judge!

PORTIA
Therefore prepare thee to cut off the flesh.
Shed thou no blood, nor cut thou less nor more
But just a pound of flesh. If thou tak'st more
Or less than a just pound, be it but so much
As makes it light or heavy in the substance   326
Or the division of the twentieth part   327
Of one poor scruple, nay, if the scale do turn   328
But in the estimation of a hair,
Thou diest, and all thy goods are confiscate.

GRATIANO
A second Daniel, a Daniel, Jew!
Now, infidel, I have you on the hip.   332

318 Soft i.e., not so fast   **319 all** nothing but   **326 substance** mass or
gross weight   **327 division** fraction   **328 scruple** 20 grains apothecaries' weight, a small quantity   **332 on the hip** i.e., at a disadvantage (a
phrase from wrestling)

PORTIA
  Why doth the Jew pause? Take thy forfeiture.
SHYLOCK
  Give me my principal, and let me go.
BASSANIO
  I have it ready for thee; here it is.
PORTIA
  He hath refused it in the open court.
  He shall have merely justice and his bond.
GRATIANO
  A Daniel, still say I, a second Daniel!
  I thank thee, Jew, for teaching me that word.
SHYLOCK
  Shall I not have barely my principal?
PORTIA
  Thou shalt have nothing but the forfeiture,
  To be so taken at thy peril, Jew.
SHYLOCK
  Why, then the devil give him good of it!
  I'll stay no longer question.   [*He starts to go.*]
PORTIA   Tarry, Jew!   344
  The law hath yet another hold on you.
  It is enacted in the laws of Venice,
  If it be proved against an alien
  That by direct or indirect attempts
  He seek the life of any citizen,
  The party 'gainst the which he doth contrive
  Shall seize one half his goods; the other half
  Comes to the privy coffer of the state,   352
  And the offender's life lies in the mercy   353
  Of the Duke only, 'gainst all other voice.
  In which predicament, I say, thou stand'st;
  For it appears, by manifest proceeding,
  That indirectly and directly too
  Thou hast contrived against the very life
  Of the defendant; and thou hast incurred
  The danger formerly by me rehearsed.   360
  Down therefore, and beg mercy of the Duke.

---

344 I'll . . . question I'll stay no further pursuing of the case **352 privy coffer** private treasury **353 lies in** lies at **360 danger . . . rehearsed** penalty already cited by me

GRATIANO

Beg that thou mayst have leave to hang thyself!
And yet, thy wealth being forfeit to the state,
Thou hast not left the value of a cord;
Therefore thou must be hanged at the state's charge.   365

DUKE

That thou shalt see the difference of our spirit,
I pardon thee thy life before thou ask it.
For half thy wealth, it is Antonio's;   368
The other half comes to the general state,
Which humbleness may drive unto a fine.   370

PORTIA

Ay, for the state, not for Antonio.   371

SHYLOCK

Nay, take my life and all! Pardon not that!
You take my house when you do take the prop
That doth sustain my house. You take my life
When you do take the means whereby I live.

PORTIA

What mercy can you render him, Antonio?

GRATIANO

A halter gratis! Nothing else, for God's sake.   377

ANTONIO

So please my lord the Duke and all the court
To quit the fine for one half of his goods,   379
I am content, so he will let me have   380
The other half in use, to render it,   381
Upon his death, unto the gentleman
That lately stole his daughter.
Two things provided more: that for this favor
He presently become a Christian;   385
The other, that he do record a gift
Here in the court of all he dies possessed   387
Unto his son Lorenzo and his daughter.

365 charge expense **368 For** as for **370 Which . . . fine** i.e., which
penitence on your part may persuade me to reduce to a fine **371 Ay
. . . Antonio** i.e., yes, the state's half may be reduced to a fine, but not
Antonio's half **377 halter** hangman's noose **379 quit** remit, relinquish,
or perhaps settle for. (That is, Antonio may ask the court to forgive even
the fine imposed in lieu of a heavier penalty.) **380 so** provided that
381 in use in trust, or possibly, to be used as a source of income **385 presently** at once **387 of . . . possessed** i.e., what remains of the portion not
placed under Antonio's trust (which will also go to Lorenzo and Jessica)

DUKE

  He shall do this, or else I do recant
  The pardon that I late pronouncèd here.

PORTIA

  Art thou contented, Jew? What dost thou say?

SHYLOCK

  I am content.

PORTIA   Clerk, draw a deed of gift.

SHYLOCK

  I pray you, give me leave to go from hence;
  I am not well. Send the deed after me,
  And I will sign it.

DUKE   Get thee gone, but do it.

GRATIANO

  In christening shalt thou have two godfathers.
  Had I been judge, thou shouldst have had ten more,   397
  To bring thee to the gallows, not to the font.

                            Exit [Shylock].

DUKE

  Sir, I entreat you home with me to dinner.

PORTIA

  I humbly do desire Your Grace of pardon.
  I must away this night toward Padua,
  And it is meet I presently set forth.

DUKE

  I am sorry that your leisure serves you not.
  Antonio, gratify this gentleman,   404
  For in my mind you are much bound to him.

                     Exeunt Duke and his train.

BASSANIO

  Most worthy gentleman, I and my friend
  Have by your wisdom been this day acquitted
  Of grievous penalties, in lieu whereof,   408
  Three thousand ducats due unto the Jew
  We freely cope your courteous pains withal.   410

                     [He offers money.]

ANTONIO

  And stand indebted over and above
  In love and service to you evermore.

---

397 ten more i.e., to make up a jury of twelve. (Jurors were colloquially termed *godfathers.*) **404 gratify** reward **408 in lieu whereof** in return for which **410 cope** requite

PORTIA

He is well paid that is well satisfied,
And I, delivering you, am satisfied
And therein do account myself well paid.
My mind was never yet more mercenary.
I pray you, know me when we meet again.
I wish you well, and so I take my leave.

[*She starts to leave.*]

BASSANIO

Dear sir, of force I must attempt you further.   419
Take some remembrance of us as a tribute,
Not as fee. Grant me two things, I pray you:
Not to deny me, and to pardon me.

PORTIA

You press me far, and therefore I will yield.
Give me your gloves; I'll wear them for your sake.   424
And, for your love, I'll take this ring from you.
Do not draw back your hand; I'll take no more,
And you in love shall not deny me this.

BASSANIO

This ring, good sir? Alas, it is a trifle!
I will not shame myself to give you this.

PORTIA

I will have nothing else but only this;
And now methinks I have a mind to it.

BASSANIO

There's more depends on this than on the value.
The dearest ring in Venice will I give you,   433
And find it out by proclamation.
Only for this, I pray you, pardon me.

PORTIA

I see, sir, you are liberal in offers.   436
You taught me first to beg, and now, methinks,
You teach me how a beggar should be answered.

BASSANIO

Good sir, this ring was given me by my wife,
And when she put it on, she made me vow
That I should neither sell nor give nor lose it.

---

419 attempt urge   **424 gloves** (Perhaps Bassanio removes his gloves, thereby revealing the ring that "Balthasar" asks of him.)   **433 dearest** most expensive   **436 liberal** generous

PORTIA
That 'scuse serves many men to save their gifts.
An if your wife be not a madwoman,
And know how well I have deserved this ring,
She would not hold out' enemy forever   445
For giving it to me. Well, peace be with you!
                          Exeunt [Portia and Nerissa].

ANTONIO
My lord Bassanio, let him have the ring.
Let his deservings and my love withal
Be valued 'gainst your wife's commandement.   449

BASSANIO
Go, Gratiano, run and overtake him;
Give him the ring, and bring him, if thou canst,
Unto Antonio's house. Away, make haste!
                          Exit Gratiano [with the ring].
Come, you and I will thither presently,
And in the morning early will we both
Fly toward Belmont. Come, Antonio.   *Exeunt.*

✦

4.2   *Enter [Portia and] Nerissa [still disguised].*

PORTIA [*Giving a deed to Nerissa*]
Inquire the Jew's house out; give him this deed   1
And let him sign it. We'll away tonight
And be a day before our husbands home.
This deed will be well welcome to Lorenzo.

        Enter Gratiano.

GRATIANO   Fair sir, you are well o'erta'en.
My lord Bassanio upon more advice   6
Hath sent you here this ring and doth entreat
Your company at dinner.   [*He gives a ring.*]
PORTIA   That cannot be.
His ring I do accept most thankfully,

---

445 would . . . out i.e., would not remain   **449 commandement** (Pronounced in four syllables.)

4.2. Location: Venice. A street.
1 deed i.e., the deed of gift   **6 advice** consideration

And so, I pray you, tell him. Furthermore,
I pray you, show my youth old Shylock's house.
GRATIANO
   That will I do.
NERISSA   Sir, I would speak with you.
   [*Aside to Portia.*] I'll see if I can get my husband's ring,
   Which I did make him swear to keep forever.
PORTIA [*Aside to Nerissa*]
   Thou mayst, I warrant. We shall have old swearing   15
   That they did give the rings away to men;
   But we'll outface them, and outswear them too.—   17
   Away, make haste! Thou know'st where I will tarry.
NERISSA
   Come, good sir, will you show me to this house?
                    [*Exeunt, Nerissa and Gratiano together,
                              Portia another way.*]

❖

15 old plenty of   **17 outface** boldly contradict

5.1

Enter Lorenzo and Jessica.

LORENZO
    The moon shines bright. In such a night as this,
    When the sweet wind did gently kiss the trees
    And they did make no noise, in such a night
    Troilus methinks mounted the Trojan walls   4
    And sighed his soul toward the Grecian tents
    Where Cressid lay that night.
JESSICA   In such a night
    Did Thisbe fearfully o'ertrip the dew,   7
    And saw the lion's shadow ere himself,
    And ran dismayed away.
LORENZO   In such a night
    Stood Dido with a willow in her hand   10
    Upon the wild sea banks, and waft her love   11
    To come again to Carthage.
JESSICA   In such a night
    Medea gathered the enchanted herbs   13
    That did renew old Aeson.
LORENZO   In such a night
    Did Jessica steal from the wealthy Jew   15
    And with an unthrift love did run from Venice   16
    As far as Belmont.
JESSICA   In such a night
    Did young Lorenzo swear he loved her well,
    Stealing her soul with many vows of faith,
    And ne'er a true one.
LORENZO   In such a night
    Did pretty Jessica, like a little shrew,
    Slander her love, and he forgave it her.

5.1. Location: Belmont. Outside Portia's house.
4 Troilus Trojan prince deserted by his beloved, Cressida, after she had
been transferred to the Greek camp   **7 Thisbe** beloved of Pyramus who,
arranging to meet him by night, was frightened by a lion. (See *A Midsummer Night's Dream*, Act 5.)   **10 Dido** Queen of Carthage, deserted by
Aeneas.   **willow** (A symbol of forsaken love.)   **11 waft** wafted, beck-
oned   **13 Medea** famous sorceress of Colchis who, after falling in love
with Jason and helping him to gain the Golden Fleece, used her magic
to restore youth to Aeson, Jason's father   **15 steal** (1) escape (2) rob
16 unthrift prodigal

JESSICA
I would out-night you, did nobody come;   23
But hark, I hear the footing of a man.   24

Enter [Stephano,] a messenger.

LORENZO
Who comes so fast in silence of the night?
STEPHANO   A friend.
LORENZO
A friend? What friend? Your name, I pray you, friend?
STEPHANO
Stephano is my name, and I bring word
My mistress will before the break of day
Be here at Belmont. She doth stray about
By holy crosses, where she kneels and prays   31
For happy wedlock hours.
LORENZO   Who comes with her?
STEPHANO
None but a holy hermit and her maid.
I pray you, is my master yet returned?
LORENZO
He is not, nor we have not heard from him.
But go we in, I pray thee, Jessica,
And ceremoniously let us prepare
Some welcome for the mistress of the house.

Enter [Launcelot, the] Clown.

LAUNCELOT   Sola, sola! Wo ha, ho! Sola, sola!   39
LORENZO   Who calls?
LAUNCELOT   Sola! Did you see Master Lorenzo? Master
Lorenzo, sola, sola!
LORENZO   Leave holloing, man! Here.
LAUNCELOT   Sola! Where, where?
LORENZO   Here.
LAUNCELOT   Tell him there's a post come from my mas-
ter, with his horn full of good news: my master will be
here ere morning.   [*Exit.*]
LORENZO
Sweet soul, let's in, and there expect their coming.   49

23 out-night i.e., outdo in the verbal games we've been playing   **24 footing** footsteps   **31 holy crosses** wayside shrines   **39 Sola** (Imitation of a
posthorn.)   **49 expect** await

And yet no matter. Why should we go in?
My friend Stephano, signify, I pray you,   51
Within the house, your mistress is at hand,
And bring your music forth into the air.

                                    [*Exit Stephano.*]

How sweet the moonlight sleeps upon this bank!
Here will we sit and let the sounds of music
Creep in our ears. Soft stillness and the night
Become the touches of sweet harmony.   57
Sit, Jessica. [*They sit.*] Look how the floor of heaven
Is thick inlaid with patens of bright gold.   59
There's not the smallest orb which thou behold'st
But in his motion like an angel sings,
Still choiring to the young-eyed cherubins;   62
Such harmony is in immortal souls,
But whilst this muddy vesture of decay   64
Doth grossly close it in, we cannot hear it.   65

        [*Enter Musicians.*]

Come, ho, and wake Diana with a hymn!   66
With sweetest touches pierce your mistress' ear
And draw her home with music.   *Play music.*

JESSICA
I am never merry when I hear sweet music.

LORENZO
The reason is, your spirits are attentive.   70
For do but note a wild and wanton herd
Or race of youthful and unhandled colts   72
Fetching mad bounds, bellowing and neighing loud,
Which is the hot condition of their blood;
If they but hear perchance a trumpet sound,
Or any air of music touch their ears,
You shall perceive them make a mutual stand,   77
Their savage eyes turned to a modest gaze

51 signify make known   **57 Become** suit.   **touches** notes (produced by
the fingering of an instrument)   **59 patens** thin, circular plates of
metal   **62 choiring** singing.   **young-eyed** eternally clear-sighted
64 muddy . . . decay i.e., mortal flesh   **65 close it in** i.e., enclose the
soul.   **hear it** i.e., hear the music of the spheres   **66 Diana** (Here,
goddess of the moon; cf. 1.2.105.)   **70 spirits are attentive** (The spirits
would be in motion within the body in merriment, whereas in sadness
they would be drawn to the heart and, as it were, busy listening.)
72 race herd   **77 mutual** common or simultaneous

By the sweet power of music. Therefore the poet 79
Did feign that Orpheus drew trees, stones, and floods, 80
Since naught so stockish, hard, and full of rage 81
But music for the time doth change his nature.
The man that hath no music in himself,
Nor is not moved with concord of sweet sounds,
Is fit for treasons, stratagems, and spoils; 85
The motions of his spirit are dull as night
And his affections dark as Erebus. 87
Let no such man be trusted. Mark the music.

    Enter Portia and Nerissa.

PORTIA
That light we see is burning in my hall.
How far that little candle throws his beams!
So shines a good deed in a naughty world. 91

NERISSA
When the moon shone, we did not see the candle.

PORTIA
So doth the greater glory dim the less.
A substitute shines brightly as a king
Until a king be by, and then his state 95
Empties itself, as doth an inland brook
Into the main of waters. Music! Hark! 97

NERISSA
It is your music, madam, of the house.

PORTIA
Nothing is good, I see, without respect. 99
Methinks it sounds much sweeter than by day.

NERISSA
Silence bestows that virtue on it, madam.

PORTIA
The crow doth sing as sweetly as the lark
When neither is attended; and I think 103
The nightingale, if she should sing by day,
When every goose is cackling, would be thought

---

79 poet possibly Ovid, with whom the story of Orpheus was a favorite
theme **80 Orpheus** legendary musician. **drew** attracted, charmed
81 stockish unfeeling **85 spoils** acts of pillage **87 Erebus** a place of
primeval darkness on the way to Hades **91 naughty** wicked **95 his**
i.e., the substitute's **97 main of waters** sea **99 respect** comparison,
context **103 neither is attended** i.e., either is alone

No better a musician than the wren.
How many things by season seasoned are   107
To their right praise and true perfection!
Peace, ho! The moon sleeps with Endymion   109
And would not be awaked.   [*The music ceases.*]

LORENZO   That is the voice,
Or I am much deceived, of Portia.

PORTIA
He knows me as the blind man knows the cuckoo,
By the bad voice.

LORENZO   Dear lady, welcome home.

PORTIA
We have been praying for our husbands' welfare,
Which speed, we hope, the better for our words.
Are they returned?

LORENZO   Madam, they are not yet;
But there is come a messenger before,
To signify their coming.

PORTIA   Go in, Nerissa.
Give order to my servants that they take
No note at all of our being absent hence;
Nor you, Lorenzo; Jessica, nor you. [*A tucket sounds.*]   121

LORENZO
Your husband is at hand. I hear his trumpet.
We are no telltales, madam, fear you not.

PORTIA
This night methinks is but the daylight sick;
It looks a little paler. 'Tis a day
Such as the day is when the sun is hid.

     *Enter Bassanio, Antonio, Gratiano, and their
     followers.*

BASSANIO
We should hold day with the Antipodes,   127
If you would walk in absence of the sun.   128

---

107 season favorable occasion   **109 Endymion** a shepherd loved by the
moon goddess, who caused him to sleep a perennial sleep in a cave on
Mount Latmos where she could visit him   **121 s.d. tucket** flourish on a
trumpet   **127–128 We . . . sun** i.e., if you, Portia, like a second sun,
would always walk about during the sun's absence, we should never
have night, but would enjoy daylight even when the Antipodes, those
who dwell on the opposite side of the globe, enjoy daylight

PORTIA

Let me give light, but let me not be light;   129
For a light wife doth make a heavy husband,   130
And never be Bassanio so for me.
But God sort all! You are welcome home, my lord.   132

BASSANIO

I thank you, madam. Give welcome to my friend.
This is the man, this is Antonio,
To whom I am so infinitely bound.

PORTIA

You should in all sense be much bound to him,   136
For, as I hear, he was much bound for you.

ANTONIO

No more than I am well acquitted of.   138

PORTIA

Sir, you are very welcome to our house.
It must appear in other ways than words;
Therefore I scant this breathing courtesy.   141

GRATIANO [*To Nerissa*]

By yonder moon I swear you do me wrong!
In faith, I gave it to the judge's clerk.
Would he were gelt that had it, for my part,   144
Since you do take it, love, so much at heart.

PORTIA

A quarrel, ho, already? What's the matter?

GRATIANO

About a hoop of gold, a paltry ring
That she did give me, whose posy was   148
For all the world like cutler's poetry
Upon a knife, "Love me, and leave me not."

NERISSA

What talk you of the posy or the value?
You swore to me, when I did give it you,
That you would wear it till your hour of death
And that it should lie with you in your grave.
Though not for me, yet for your vehement oaths,
You should have been respective and have kept it.   156

---

129 be light be wanton, unchaste   **130 heavy** sad   **132 sort** decide,
dispose   **136 in all sense** in every way, with every reason   **138 acquitted of** repaid for   **141 scant . . . courtesy** make brief this empty (i.e.,
merely verbal) courtesy   **144 gelt** gelded.   **for my part** as far as I'm
concerned   **148 posy** a motto on a ring   **156 respective** mindful

Gave it a judge's clerk! No, God's my judge,
The clerk will ne'er wear hair on 's face that had it.

GRATIANO
He will, an if he live to be a man.   159

NERISSA
Ay, if a woman live to be a man.

GRATIANO
Now, by this hand, I gave it to a youth,
A kind of boy, a little scrubbèd boy,   162
No higher than thyself, the judge's clerk,
A prating boy, that begged it as a fee.   164
I could not for my heart deny it him.

PORTIA
You were to blame—I must be plain with you—
To part so slightly with your wife's first gift,
A thing stuck on with oaths upon your finger,
And so riveted with faith unto your flesh.
I gave my love a ring and made him swear
Never to part with it; and here he stands.
I dare be sworn for him he would not leave it,
Nor pluck it from his finger, for the wealth
That the world masters. Now, in faith, Gratiano,   174
You give your wife too unkind a cause of grief.
An 'twere to me, I should be mad at it.   176

BASSANIO [*Aside*]
Why, I were best to cut my left hand off
And swear I lost the ring defending it.

GRATIANO
My lord Bassanio gave his ring away
Unto the judge that begged it and indeed
Deserved it too; and then the boy, his clerk,
That took some pains in writing, he begged mine;
And neither man nor master would take aught   183
But the two rings.

PORTIA   What ring gave you, my lord?
Not that, I hope, which you received of me.

BASSANIO
If I could add a lie unto a fault,
I would deny it; but you see my finger

159 an if if   162 scrubbèd stunted   164 prating chattering
174 masters owns   176 An if.   mad beside myself   183 aught anything

Hath not the ring upon it. It is gone.

PORTIA
Even so void is your false heart of truth.
By heaven, I will ne'er come in your bed
Until I see the ring!

NERISSA   Nor I in yours
Till I again see mine.

BASSANIO   Sweet Portia,
If you did know to whom I gave the ring,
If you did know for whom I gave the ring,
And would conceive for what I gave the ring,
And how unwillingly I left the ring,
When naught would be accepted but the ring,
You would abate the strength of your displeasure.

PORTIA
If you had known the virtue of the ring,   199
Or half her worthiness that gave the ring,
Or your own honor to contain the ring,   201
You would not then have parted with the ring.
What man is there so much unreasonable,
If you had pleased to have defended it
With any terms of zeal, wanted the modesty   205
To urge the thing held as a ceremony?   206
Nerissa teaches me what to believe:
I'll die for 't but some woman had the ring.

BASSANIO
No, by my honor, madam! By my soul,
No woman had it, but a civil doctor,   210
Which did refuse three thousand ducats of me
And begged the ring, the which I did deny him
And suffered him to go displeased away—
Even he that had held up the very life
Of my dear friend. What should I say, sweet lady?
I was enforced to send it after him.
I was beset with shame and courtesy.
My honor would not let ingratitude
So much besmear it. Pardon me, good lady!
For by these blessèd candles of the night,   220

---

199 virtue power **201 contain** retain **205 wanted the modesty** who
would have been so lacking in consideration as **206 urge** insist upon
receiving. **ceremony** something sacred **210 civil doctor** i.e., doctor of
civil law **220 blessèd . . . night** i.e., stars

Had you been there, I think you would have begged
The ring of me to give the worthy doctor.

PORTIA
Let not that doctor e'er come near my house.
Since he hath got the jewel that I loved,
And that which you did swear to keep for me,
I will become as liberal as you: 226
I'll not deny him anything I have,
No, not my body nor my husband's bed.
Know him I shall, I am well sure of it.
Lie not a night from home. Watch me like Argus;   230
If you do not, if I be left alone,
Now, by mine honor, which is yet mine own,
I'll have that doctor for my bedfellow.

NERISSA
And I his clerk; therefore be well advised
How you do leave me to mine own protection.

GRATIANO
Well, do you so. Let not me take him, then!   236
For if I do, I'll mar the young clerk's pen.   237

ANTONIO
I am th' unhappy subject of these quarrels.

PORTIA
Sir, grieve not you; you are welcome notwithstanding.

BASSANIO
Portia, forgive me this enforcèd wrong,
And in the hearing of these many friends
I swear to thee, even by thine own fair eyes
Wherein I see myself—

PORTIA   Mark you but that!
In both my eyes he doubly sees himself;
In each eye, one. Swear by your double self,   245
And there's an oath of credit.

BASSANIO   Nay, but hear me.   246
Pardon this fault, and by my soul I swear
I never more will break an oath with thee.

ANTONIO
I once did lend my body for his wealth,   249

___

226 liberal generous (sexually as well as otherwise) **230 from** away
from. **Argus** mythological monster with a hundred eyes **236 take**
apprehend **237 pen** (with sexual double meaning) **245 double** i.e.,
deceitful **246 of credit** worthy to be believed **249 wealth** welfare

Which, but for him that had your husband's ring,
Had quite miscarried. I dare be bound again,
My soul upon the forfeit, that your lord
Will never more break faith advisedly.   253

PORTIA
Then you shall be his surety. Give him this,   254
And bid him keep it better than the other.
                      [*She gives the ring to Antonio, who*
                              gives it to Bassanio.]

ANTONIO
Here, Lord Bassanio. Swear to keep this ring.

BASSANIO
By heaven, it is the same I gave the doctor!

PORTIA
I had it of him. Pardon me, Bassanio,
For by this ring the doctor lay with me.

NERISSA
And pardon me, my gentle Gratiano,
For that same scrubbèd boy, the doctor's clerk,
In lieu of this last night did lie with me.   262
                      [*Presenting her ring.*]

GRATIANO
Why, this is like the mending of highways
In summer, where the ways are fair enough.   264
What, are wc cuckolds ere we have deserved it?   265

PORTIA
Speak not so grossly. You are all amazed.   266
Here is a letter; read it at your leisure.[*She gives a letter.*]
It comes from Padua, from Bellario.
There you shall find that Portia was the doctor,
Nerissa there her clerk. Lorenzo here
Shall witness I set forth as soon as you,
And even but now returned; I have not yet
Entered my house. Antonio, you are welcome,
And I have better news in store for you
Than you expect. Unseal this letter soon.
                      [*She gives him a letter.*]
There you shall find three of your argosies

---

253 advisedly intentionally   **254 surety** guarantor   **262 In lieu of** in
return for   **264 In . . . enough** i.e., before repair is necessary
265 cuckolds husbands whose wives are unfaithful   **266 grossly** stu-
pidly, licentiously.   **amazed** bewildered

Are richly come to harbor suddenly.
You shall not know by what strange accident
I chancèd on this letter.

ANTONIO   I am dumb.

BASSANIO
Were you the doctor and I knew you not?

GRATIANO
Were you the clerk that is to make me cuckold?

NERISSA
Ay, but the clerk that never means to do it,
Unless he live until he be a man.

BASSANIO
Sweet doctor, you shall be my bedfellow.
When I am absent, then lie with my wife.

ANTONIO
Sweet lady, you have given me life and living;
For here I read for certain that my ships
Are safely come to road.

PORTIA   How now, Lorenzo?   288
My clerk hath some good comforts too for you.

NERISSA
Ay, and I'll give them him without a fee.
                    [*She gives a deed.*]
There do I give to you and Jessica,
From the rich Jew, a special deed of gift,
After his death, of all he dies possessed of.

LORENZO
Fair ladies, you drop manna in the way   294
Of starvèd people.

PORTIA   It is almost morning,
And yet I am sure you are not satisfied
Of these events at full. Let us go in;
And charge us there upon inter'gatories,   298
And we will answer all things faithfully.

GRATIANO
Let it be so. The first inter'gatory
That my Nerissa shall be sworn on is,

288 road anchorage   **294 manna** the food miraculously supplied to the
Israelites in the wilderness (Exodus 16)   **298 charge . . . inter'gatories**
require ourselves to answer all things under oath

Whether till the next night she had rather stay   302
Or go to bed now, being two hours to day.
But were the day come, I should wish it dark
Till I were couching with the doctor's clerk.
Well, while I live I'll fear no other thing
So sore as keeping safe Nerissa's ring.   *Exeunt.* 307

302 stay wait   **307 ring** (with sexual suggestion)

Date and Text

The Stationers' Register, the official record book of the London Company of Stationers (booksellers and printers), for July 22, 1598, contains an entry on behalf of the printer James Roberts for "a booke of the Marchaunt of Venyce, or otherwise called the Jewe of Venyce, Prouided, that yt bee not prynted by the said James Robertes or anye other whatsoeuer without lycence first had from the Right honorable the lord Chamberlen." Roberts evidently enjoyed a close connection with the Chamberlain's men (Shakespeare's acting company) and seemingly was granted the special favor of registering the play at this time even though the company did not wish to see the play published until later. In 1600, at any rate, Roberts transferred his rights as publisher to Thomas Heyes and printed the volume for him with the following title:

> The most excellent Historie of the *Merchant of Venice*. VVith the extreme crueltie of *Shylocke* the Iewe towards the sayd Merchant, in cutting a iust pound of his flesh: and the obtayning of *Portia* by the choyse of three chests. *As it hath beene diuers times acted by the Lord Chamberlaine his Seruants*. Written by William Shakespeare. AT LONDON, Printed by *I. R.* [James Roberts] for Thomas Heyes, and are to be sold in Paules Church-yard, at the signe of the Greene Dragon. 1600.

The text of this 1600 quarto is generally a good one, based seemingly on the author's papers. It served as copy for the second quarto of 1619 (printed by William Jaggard for Thomas Pavier, and fraudulently dated 1600) and for the First Folio of 1623. The Folio stage directions may represent some authoritative consultation of a theatrical document.

Francis Meres mentions the play in 1598 in his *Palladis Tamia: Wit's Treasury* (a slender volume on contemporary literature and art; valuable because it lists most of Shakespeare's plays that existed at that time). Establishing an earlier limit for dating has proven not so easy. Many scholars have urged a connection with the Roderigo Lopez affair of 1594 (see the Introduction to the play). The supposed allusion to Lopez in the lines about "a wolf, who, hanged for human slaughter" (4.1.134) may simply indicate, however, that wolves were actually hanged for attacking men in Shakespeare's day (as dogs were for killing sheep). Besides, the Lopez case remained so notorious throughout the 1590s that even a proven allusion to it in *The Merchant* would not limit the play to 1594 or 1595. Christopher Marlowe's play *The Jew of Malta* was revived in 1594 to exploit anti-Lopez sentiment but was also revived in 1596. There may, on the other hand, be an allusion in 1.1.27 to the *St. Andrew,* a Spanish ship captured at Cadiz in 1596. Any date between 1594 and early 1598 is possible, though the latter half of this period is more likely.

Textual Notes

These textual notes are not an historical collation, either of the early quarto and the early folios or of more recent editions; they are simply a record of departures in this edition from the copy text. The reading adopted in this edition appears in boldface, followed by the rejected reading from the copy text, i.e., the quarto of 1600. Only major alterations in punctuation are noted. Changes in lineation are not indicated, nor are some minor and obvious typographical errors.

Abbreviations used:
Q quarto
s.d. stage direction
s.p. speech prefix

Copy text: the first quarto of 1600 [Q1].

1.1. s.d. [and elsewhere] Salerio, and Solanio Salaryno, and Salanio
19 Peering Piring   **27 docked** docks   **85 jaundice** jaundies   **112 tongue** togue   **113 Is** It is   **128 off** of   **151 back** bake

1.2. 44 Palatine Palentine [and at ll. 57–58]   **53 Bon** Boune   **58 throstle** Trassell   **119 s.d. Enter a Servingman** [after l. 120 in Q1]

1.3. 28 s.p. [and elsewhere] Shylock Jew   **76 compromised** compremyzd
110 spit spet [also at ll. 124 and 129]

2.1. s.d. Morocco Morochus   **25 Sophy . . . prince,** Sophy, and a Persian Prince   **31 thee** the   **35 page** rage

2.2. 1 s.p. [and elsewhere] Launcelot Clowne   **3 [and elsewhere in this scene] Gobbo** Iobbe   **42 By** Be   **76 murder** muder   **94 last** lost   **165 s.d. Exit Leonardo** [after l. 164 in Q1]   **168 a suit** sute

2.3. 11 did doe

2.4. 39 s.d. Exeunt Exit

2.6. 26 Who's whose [also at l. 61]   **35 night, you** night you   **59 gentlemen** gentleman

2.7. 18 threatens. Men threatens men   **45 Spits** Spets   **69 tombs** timber

2.8. 8 gondola Gondylo   **39 Slubber** slumber

2.9. 64 judgment iudement

3.1. 21 s.d. Enter Shylock [after l. 22 in Q1]   **70 s.p. Man** [not in Q1]   **74 s.d.** [Q1 repeats the s.d. "Enter Tuball"]   **100 Heard** heere   **114 turquoise** Turkies

3.2. 61 live. With liue with   **67 eyes** eye   **81 vice** voyce   **84 stairs** stayers
199 loved; for intermission lou'd for intermission,   **204 roof** rough
315 s.p. Bassanio [not in Q1]

3.3. s.d. Solanio Salerio   **24 s.p. Solanio** Sal

3.4. 49 Padua Mantua   **50 cousin's** cosin   **53 traject** Tranect   **80 near**
nere   **81 my** my my

3.5. 20 e'en in   **26 comes** come   **74 merit it** meane it, it   **81 a wife** wife
87 s.d. Exeunt Exit

4.1. 30 his state this states   **31 flint** flints   **35 s.p. [and elsewhere in this
scene] Shylock** Jew   **50 urine; for affection,** vrine for affection.   **51 Mistress**
Maisters   **73 You may as well** well   **74 Why he hath made the** the   **bleat**
bleake   **75 pines** of Pines   **100 is** as   **113 lose** loose   **136 whilst** whilest
228 No, not Not not   **270 off** of   **322 off** of   **396 s.p. Gratiano** Shy   **405 s.d.
Exeunt** Exit

5.1. 26 s.p. Stephano Messen [also at ll. 28 and 33]   **41 Lorenzo** Lorenzo,
&   **49 Sweet soul** [assigned in Q1 to Launcelot]   **51 Stephano** Stephen
87 Erebus Terebus   **109 ho** how   **152 give it** giue   **233 my** mine

Shakespeare's Sources

Shakespeare's probable chief source for *The Merchant of Venice* was the first story of the fourth day of *Il Pecorone* (The Dunce), by Ser Giovanni Fiorentino. This collection of tales dates from the late fourteenth century but was first published in 1558 at Milan and was not published in English translation in Shakespeare's time. If Shakespeare was unable to read it in Italian, he may conceivably have consulted a translation in some now-lost manuscript; such translations did sometimes circulate. Behind Ser Giovanni's story lies an old tradition of a bond given for human flesh, as found in Persia, India, and the Twelve Tables of Roman Law. This legend first appears in English in the thirteenth-century *Cursor Mundi* (a long verse history of the world from creation to doomsday), with a Jew as the creditor. A thirteenth-century version of the *Gesta Romanorum* (a popular collection of stories in Latin) adds a romantic love plot; the evil moneylender in this story is not Jewish. The hero pawns his own flesh to a merchant in order to win a lady. He succeeds on his third attempt, having learned to avoid a magic spell that had previously put him to sleep and cost him a large number of florins. When he goes to pay his forfeit, the lady follows him disguised as a knight and foils the evil merchant by pointing out a quibbling distinction between flesh and blood.

Il Pecorone, presented here in a new and complete translation, provided Shakespeare with a number of essential elements, although not all that he included in his play. Ser Giovanni's story tells of Giannetto, the adventurous youngest son of a Florentine merchant, who goes to live with his father's dearest friend, Ansaldo, in Venice. This worthy merchant gives him money to seek his fortune at sea. Unbeknownst to Ansaldo, Giannetto twice risks everything to woo the lady of Belmont: if he can succeed in sleeping with her, he will win her and her country, but if he fails, he loses all his wealth. Twice Giannetto is given a sleeping medicine in his wine and has to forfeit everything. Returning destitute to Venice twice, he is reunited each time with Ansaldo and given the means to seek his fortune again. For the third such voyage, however, Ansaldo is driven to borrow ten thousand florins from a Jew, using the forfeiture of a pound of flesh as a guarantee. This time, one of the lady's maids warns Giannetto not to drink his wine, and he finally possesses the lady as his wife. Sometime later, remembering that the day of Ansaldo's forfeiture has arrived, Giannetto explains the predicament to his wife and is sent by her to Venice with a hundred thousand florins, but he arrives after the forfeiture has fallen due. The lady, however, following after him in the disguise of a doctor of laws, decrees that the Jew may have no blood and must take no more or no less than one pound of flesh. The Jew is jeered at and receives no money. The "doctor of laws" refuses any payment other than the ring Giannetto was given by his lady. Yielding it up unwillingly, he returns to Belmont, where his lady vexes him about the ring but finally relents and tells him all. Shakespeare could thus have found in one source the wooing, the borrowing from a Jewish moneylender, the pound of flesh, the trial, and the business of the rings. The story provides no casket episode, courtship of Nerissa by Gratiano, elopement of Jessica, or clowning of Launcelot Gobbo. The Jew's motive is not prompted by the way he has been treated.

Shakespeare may also have known "The Ballad of Gernutus," a popular English work that seems to be older than the play. It has no love plot but dwells on the unnatural cruelty of a Jewish Venetian usurer who takes a bond of flesh for "a merry jest." Anthony Munday's prose *Zelauto* (1580), though its villain is a Christian rather than a Jewish moneylender, also features a bond of this sort, taken purportedly as a mere sport but with hidden malice. Truculento, the villain, takes the bond of two young men, Rodolfo and his friend Strabino, as surety for a loan. If they forfeit the loan, the young men are to lose their lands and their right eyes as well. The villain has a daughter, Brisana, whom he permits to marry Rodolfo since Truculento expects to marry Rodolfo's sister Cornelia himself. When Cornelia instead marries Strabino, Truculento angrily takes the young men to court to demand his bond. The two brides disguise themselves as scholars and go to court, where they appeal for mercy and then foil Truculento by means of the legal quibble about blood.

Another possible source for the courtroom scene is *The Orator*, translated into English in 1596 from the French of Alexandre Sylvain. An oration, entitled "Of a Jew, who would for his debt have a pound of the flesh of a Christian," uses many specious arguments also employed by Shylock, and is forthrightly confuted in "The Christian's Answer."

Shylock's relationship to his daughter finds obvious earlier parallels in *Zelauto* and in Christopher Marlowe's play *The Jew of Malta* (c. 1589), in which Barabas's daughter Abigail loves a Christian and ultimately renounces her faith. The actual elopement, however, is closer to the fourteenth story in Masuccio of Salerno's fifteenth-century *Il Novellino* (not published in English translation in Shakespeare's day).

The casket-choosing episode, not found in *Il Pecorone*, was a widespread legend, occurring for example in the story of *Barlaam and Josophat* (ninth-century Greek, translated into Latin by the thirteenth century), in Vincent of Beauvais's *Speculum Historiale*, in the *Legenda Aurea*, in Giovanni Boccaccio's *Decameron* (Day 10, Story 1), in John Gower's *Confessio Amantis*, and—closest to Shakespeare—in the *Gesta Romanorum* (translated into English in 1577 by Richard Robinson and "bettered" by him in 1595). In this last account, the choice is between a gold, silver, and lead casket, each with its own inscription. The first two inscriptions are like Shakespeare's; the third reads, "They that choose me, shall find [in] me that God hath disposed." The chooser, however, is a maiden, and she is not preceded by other contestants.

An old play called *The Jew* is referred to by Stephen Gosson in 1579 as containing "the greediness of worldly choosers, and bloody minds of usurers." Scholars have speculated that this was a source play for Shakespeare, but actually we have too little to go on to make a reliable judgment. Gosson was surely not referring to Robert Wilson's *The Three Ladies of London* (c. 1581) in any case, even though it is sometimes suggested as an analogue to *The Merchant of Venice*, for its Jewish figure named Gerontus (compare Gernutus in the ballad) is an exemplary person. Besides, the probable date of this play is later than Gosson's remark.

Il Pecorone

By Ser Giovanni Fiorentino
Translated by David Bevington and Kate Bevington

FOURTH DAY, FIRST STORY: GIANNETTO
AND THE LADY OF BELMONT

There once was in Florence, in the house of the Scali, a merchant named Bindo, who had been to Tana and to Alexandria many times, and on all the usual long voyages that are
made for the sake of merchandise. This Bindo was very
rich, and he had three strapping sons. As he was approaching death, he summoned the eldest and the middle son and,
in their presence, made his last will and testament, desig-
nating the two of them heirs of all he had in the world, and
making no mention of his youngest son.

When he had made his will, his youngest son, named
Giannetto, hearing of this, went to him in his bed and said,
"Father, I am much amazed at what you have done, not to
have remembered me in your will."

"Giannetto," his father answered, "there is no creature
in the world whom I hold dearer than you. And for that reason I do not want you to stay here after my death, but wish
instead that you go to Venice when I am dead, to your godfather, Signor Ansaldo, who has no son of his own and who
has many times written me to send you to him. I can tell you
that he is the richest merchant today in all Christendom. So
I want you, when I am dead, to go to him and take this letter;
if you behave wisely, you will become a rich man."

"Father," the young man said, "I am ready to do what
you command me."

Then the father gave him his blessing, and a few days
later he died. All the sons lamented bitterly and gave to the
body the ceremonies that were its due.

A few days later the two brothers summoned Giannetto
and said, "Brother, it is true that our father made his will
and left us his heirs, and did not mention you; nonetheless,
you are our brother, and whatever we have is also yours as
long as it lasts."

"Brothers," answered Giannetto, "I thank you for your

offer, but, as for me, I intend to seek my fortune elsewhere. My mind is made up on this, so let the inheritance be yours by right of law and with our father's blessing."

The brothers, seeing that his mind was made up, gave him a horse and money for expenses. Giannetto took leave of them and went to Venice, and, arriving at the counting-house of Signor Ansaldo, presented him with the letter his father had given him before his death. Signor Ansaldo, as he read the letter, realized that this was the son of his dearest friend, Bindo; and when he had finished the letter, he at once embraced the young man, saying, "Welcome, my son, whom I have so much desired to see." And immediately he asked about Bindo, to which Giannetto replied that he was dead. With many tears Signor Ansaldo embraced and kissed Giannetto, and said, "I am very grieved at the death of Bindo, for it was he who helped me earn a great part of what I have; but the happiness that I have in seeing you is so great that it takes away some of my sorrow." And he had him conducted to his house, and told his clerks and attendants and servants and grooms and whoever else belonged to the household that Giannetto was to be obeyed and served more than his own self. He consigned to him the keys to all his ready money and said, "My son, whatever there is is yours; spend it on clothes today as you please; keep a table for the important people of the city, and become known. For I leave this thought with you: The more you win others' good will, the more I will love you."

And so Giannetto began to enter into Venetian society, to dine out and give dinner parties, to make gifts, to keep liveried servants, to buy fine horses, and to take part in jousts and tournaments, for he was expert and well versed in such matters and magnanimous and gracious in all things, knowing well how to show respect and courtesy as was fitting; and always he honored Signor Ansaldo more than if he had been a hundred times his father. So sensible was his behavior toward persons of all conditions that virtually everyone in Venice liked him, seeing him to be so wise and pleasing in manner and courteous beyond measure. Women and men alike were quite taken with him, and Signor Ansaldo had eyes for no one but him, so pleasing were his behavior and his manners. Scarcely a party went by to which Giannetto was not invited, so well was he liked by one and all.

Now, it happened that two dear friends of his planned to make a voyage to Alexandria with their two ships and their merchandise, as they did each year. They spoke of this to Giannetto and asked if he wished to enjoy himself by going with them to see the world, especially Damascus and the region where it lies.

"In good faith," answered Giannetto, "I would very much like to go, if my father Signor Ansaldo gives me his permission."

"We'll see to it that he does," they said, "and that he will be content."

And so right away they went to Signor Ansaldo and said, "We want to ask you please to give your permission for Giannetto to go next spring with us to Alexandria, and to furnish him with some kind of ship so that he can see a little of the world."

"I am content," said Signor Ansaldo, "if he wants to."

"Sir," said they, "he does."

So Signor Ansaldo at once had him furnished with a splendid ship and arranged for it to be loaded with a great deal of merchandise and decked out with flags and provided with whatever arms were needed. And when all was ready, Signor Ansaldo ordered the captain and those others who served on board that they were to do what Giannetto commanded them and that his safety was in their hands. "For," said Signor Ansaldo, "I am not sending him out for any profits that I want him to make, but rather for him to enjoy himself and see something of the world."

When Giannetto was about to leave, all Venice gathered to see, for not in a long while had so magnificent and well equipped a vessel sailed from Venice. Everyone was sorry at his departure. He took leave of Signor Ansaldo and of all his friends, then put out to sea, hoisted sail, and set his course for Alexandria in the name of God and good fortune.

As the three friends in their three ships were sailing along day after day, early one morning, before it was broad daylight, Giannetto looked out and saw a most splendid harbor in a gulf of the sea, and asked the captain what it was called.

"Sir," the captain answered, "that harbor belongs to a widowed lady, one who has meant trouble for a lot of gentlemen."

"How?" said Giannetto.

"Sir," said the other, "the truth is that she is a beautiful woman, and enchanting too, and she has established this law: Whatever man arrives there must sleep with her, and if he succeeds in enjoying her, he is to take her as his wife and be lord of the whole country, but if he does not succeed in enjoying her, he loses everything that he has in the world."

Giannetto thought about that for a bit, and then said, "Devise any means you can to bring me into that harbor."

"Sir," the captain said, "take care what you say, for many gentlemen have gone there only to lose all their goods and their lives in the bargain."

"Don't interfere," said Giannetto. "Do what I tell you."

And so it was done. Quickly they changed the ship's course and brought her to berth in that harbor, without his friends in the other ships seeing a thing. Now, when morning came, the news spread that this splendid ship had arrived in the harbor; everybody gathered to see it, and the news was brought to the lady, who sent for Giannetto. He went to her at once, and greeted her with great respect. She took him by the hand and asked who he was and where he was from, and if he knew the custom of the country.

Giannetto replied that he did, and that he had come for no other reason.

"You are a hundred times welcome," she said.

She paid him great honor all that day, and had many barons, counts, and knights who were her subjects invited to attend on him. The manners of this young man delighted all the barons, so well educated was he, so pleasing of person, and so well spoken, and nearly everybody was taken with him. All that day there was dancing and singing and festivity at the court as an expression of affection for him, and everyone would have been well content to have him as lord.

Now, as evening approached, the lady took him by the hand and led him into her room, and said, "It seems to me that it's time to go to bed."

"My lady," said Giannetto, "I am at your service."

Immediately two damsels came into the room, one with wine and the other with sweetmeats.

"You must be thirsty," said the lady. "Have something to drink."

Giannetto took some of the sweetmeats and drank some

wine, which had been drugged to make him sleep, though he didn't know this, and so he drank half a glass, since it seemed good to him. Immediately he undressed and went to lie down. And as soon as he reached the bed, he fell sound asleep. The lady lay down at his side, but he was out for the rest of the night, until nine o'clock. The lady, as soon as it was day, arose and gave orders to unload the ship, and found it full of rich and worthy merchandise. When it was nine o'clock, the lady's maidservants went to the bed, roused Giannetto, and told him to begone with God's blessing, for he had lost his ship and all that was in it. He was ashamed and realized he had done badly. The lady gave him money for expenses and a horse, which he mounted, and, sad and gloomy, he made his way toward Venice. Arriving there, he was too ashamed to want to go home to Signor Ansaldo, and so by night he went to the house of a friend.

This friend marveled at him and said, "Giannetto, what happened?"

"My ship struck a rock one night," he answered, "and split apart and scattered every which way. I lashed myself to a timber that cast me ashore, and so I have come home on dry land, and here I am."

He remained several days hidden in the house of his friend.

One day this friend paid a visit to Signor Ansaldo and found him very melancholy. "What's wrong," he said, "that you are so downhearted?"

"I'm greatly afraid," said Signor Ansaldo, "that my son is dead, or that the sea has brought him misfortune. I can find no peace of mind or happiness until I see him again, so great is the love I bear him."

"Sir," said the young man, "I can tell you news of him, which is that he was shipwrecked and lost everything, but saved himself."

"Praised be God!" said Signor Ansaldo. "If he is saved, I am happy. As to what he lost, I don't care at all." And immediately he got up and went off to see Giannetto. And when he saw him, immediately he ran to embrace him, and said, "My son, there is no need for you to be ashamed as far as I am concerned. Shipwrecks happen all the time. So, my son, don't be downcast. As long as no harm has come to you, I am happy." And he led him home, comforting him all the while. The news spread through all Venice, and everyone felt sorry for the loss that Giannetto had suffered.

Now, it happened that a short time later the two friends of Giannetto came back from Alexandria, very wealthy. And when they arrived, they inquired after Giannetto and were told the whole business. At once they ran to greet him, saying, "How did you get separated, or where did you go, that we were unable to get any news of you? We doubled back on our track all day long, but could never see you or find out where you had gone. And we were so sorry about this that all our journey we could not succeed in cheering ourselves up, thinking you were dead."

"A wind came up in a gulf of the sea," Giannetto answered, "and drove my ship against a rock close to the shore. I hardly was able to save myself, and everything was scattered."

Such was the excuse that Giannetto gave in order not to reveal his error. Together they made a great feast, thanking God that he had been saved, saying, "Next spring, God willing, we will make enough profit to recover what you have lost this time, but now let's give ourselves a good time without any gloominess." And so they devoted themselves to pleasure and enjoyment, as they used to do.

But Giannetto did nothing but think about how he might return to that lady, dreaming of this and saying to himself, "Certainly I must have her for my wife, or I will die," and for the most part he could not be merry.

Signor Ansaldo said to him many times, "My son, don't give yourself up to melancholy. We have goods enough to live very well."

"My lord," answered Giannetto, "I can never be content unless I make that journey again."

Seeing that his mind was made up, Signor Ansaldo, when it was time, fitted out another ship for him with much more merchandise and of better value than before. And he began so early that, when the time finally came, the ship was well furnished and adorned. He gave for it the greater part of all that he had in the world. The friends, when they had fitted out their ships with what they needed, put out to sea, hoisted sail, and set forth on their voyage.

They sailed along for several days, and Giannetto constantly kept a lookout, to see once more the harbor of that lady, which was called the Harbor of the Lady of Belmont. Arriving one night at the mouth of the harbor, which was in a gulf of the sea, Giannetto recognized it at once, had the sails and the rudder brought about, and berthed within the harbor.

The lady, when she arose in the morning, looked down to the harbor and saw the flags of that ship flying. At once she recognized it, and summoned a maidservant and said, "Do you recognize those flags?"

"My lady," said the maidservant, "it seems to me they are the insignia of the young man who arrived here a year ago and who brought such an abundance of riches with his merchandise."

"Certainly what you say is true," said the lady, "and truly this is no ordinary matter; truly he must be in love with me, for I never saw anyone come back a second time."

"I never saw a more courteous and graceful man than he," said the maidservant.

The lady sent many damsels and squires for him, who greeted him with great festivity; and he treated all of them with cheerfulness and joy. And so he came into the presence of the lady. When she saw him, she embraced him with joy and delight, and he embraced her with reverential courtesy. They passed all that day in revelry and pleasure, for the lady sent invitations to many barons and ladies, who came to her court to celebrate in Giannetto's honor. Almost all the barons were full of regret and gladly would have had him for their lord, because of his amiability and liberality, and almost all the ladies were in love with him, seeing with what skill he led the dancing and that he held his countenance always cheerful, so that everyone believed him to be the son of some great nobleman.

When it came time for sleep, the lady took Giannetto by the hand and said, "Let us go and lie down." They went to her room and sat down, and behold, two damsels came with wine and sweetmeats, and the couple drank and ate, and then they went to bed. And as soon as Giannetto was in bed, he fell sound asleep. The lady undressed and lay down beside him, and—to be brief—he was out for the whole night. And when morning came, the lady arose and immediately ordered the unloading of the ship. When it was nine o'clock,

Giannetto came to his senses and looked about for the lady but could not find her. He lifted up his head and saw that it was broad daylight, and so got up and began to feel ashamed. He was given a horse and money for expenses and quickly departed, sad and gloomy, and he did not rest until he was at Venice. By night he went to the house of his friend, who, on seeing him, was the most astonished person in the world, saying, "What happened?"

"Things are bad with me," said Giannetto. "Accursed be the fortune that ever brought me to this country!"

"Certainly you have reason to curse your fortune," said his friend, "for you have ruined Signor Ansaldo, who was the greatest and richest merchant in Christendom, and the shame of that is worse than the loss."

For several days Giannetto remained hidden in his friend's house, not knowing what to do or to say. He almost decided to go back to Florence without saying a word to Signor Ansaldo, but in the end he made up his mind to go to him, and so he did.

When Signor Ansaldo saw him, he got up and ran and embraced him, saying, "Welcome, my dear son." And Giannetto, weeping, embraced him. Signor Ansaldo said, "Do you know what? Do not give yourself the slightest grief. Since I have you once again, I am happy. There is still enough remaining for us to be able to live simply."

The news of what had happened went all over Venice, and everyone talked of Signor Ansaldo, wishing him well and grieving for what he had suffered. And it was necessary for him to sell many of his possessions to pay his creditors who had provided him with the lost merchandise.

Now, it happened that Giannetto's two friends returned, rich from their journey, and arrived in Venice, where they were told that Giannetto had come back having been shipwrecked and having lost everything. They marveled at this, saying, "This is the most amazing thing ever seen." And they went to Signor Ansaldo and Giannetto in a jovial mood, saying, "Signors, don't be downcast, for we intend to go this coming year and make a profit on your behalf. After all, we are partly responsible for your loss, since we are the ones who induced Giannetto to come with us in the first place. Don't worry. As long as we have any goods ourselves, treat them as your own."

Signor Ansaldo thanked them and said that he still had enough to get by on.

Now, it happened that Giannetto, thinking day and night on what had taken place, could not bring himself to be cheerful. Signor Ansaldo asked him what was the matter.

"I shall never be content," he said, "until I have gotten back what I lost."

"My son," said Signor Ansaldo, "I don't want you to go away any more, for it is better that we live here simply, with what little we have, than that you again undertake such a risky journey."

"I am firmly resolved to do what I've said," said Giannetto, "for I would consider myself in a shameful state if I left things as they are."

Signor Ansaldo, seeing that his mind was made up, made arrangements to sell everything he had in the world and fit out another ship for him. And he did this, so that he had nothing left, and fitted out a magnificent ship with merchandise. Because he still needed ten thousand florins, he went to a Jew at Mestre and borrowed the money on these terms and conditions: If he had not repaid him by St. John's Day in the following June, the said Jew should have the right to take a pound of his flesh from whatever part of the body he pleased. Signor Ansaldo was content with this, and so the Jew had a deed drawn up for the purpose, authenticated by witnesses and with those forms and ceremonies pertaining in such a case; and then he counted out ten thousand gold florins. With this money Signor Ansaldo supplied what was still lacking for the ship; and if the other two were fine, this one was much richer and better equipped. And so the friends did the same for their two ships, having it in mind that whatever profit they made would be for Giannetto. When it came time for departure, Signor Ansaldo said to Giannetto, "My son, you are going away, and you know how things stand with me. One favor I ask of you: If you come to grief, please come see me, so that I can see you again before I die, and I will depart content." Giannetto promised him this, and Signor Ansaldo gave him his blessing. And so the three took their leave and set off on their voyage.

The two friends kept a constant eye on Giannetto's ship. Giannetto meanwhile was always watching to see how he might drop into the harbor of Belmont. And so he made a deal with one of the sailors that one night the man would pilot the ship into the harbor of that lady. When the morning light grew clear, his friends in the other two ships looked about them, but nowhere did they see Giannetto's ship. They said to each other, "Bad luck again, for sure!" And they decided to keep on their way, wondering greatly all the while.

Now, it happened that when the ship came into the harbor, the whole city drew near to see, realizing that Giannetto had returned. They marveled greatly at this, saying, "Certainly this must be the son of some very important man, seeing how he comes here each year with so much merchandise and so beautiful a ship. Would to God he were our lord!" And so he was waited on by all the dignitaries, barons, and knights of that city.

Word was brought to the lady that Giannetto had come. She placed herself at a window and saw the handsome ship and recognized the flags. Whereupon she made the sign of the cross, saying, "Certainly this is the same man who brought such riches into this country," and she sent for him. Giannetto came to her, and with many embraces they greeted each other and offered their respects. And the whole day was spent amid joy and festivity. For love of Giannetto a splendid joust was held, and many barons and knights jousted that day. Giannetto wanted to joust also, and that day he performed many miraculous feats himself, so skillful was he in arms and horsemanship. So much did his conduct please all the barons that everyone wanted him to be their lord.

Now, when evening came and it was time for bed, the lady took Giannetto by the hand and said, "Let us go and rest."

And as he was about to leave the room, one of the maid-servants, feeling sorry for Giannetto, whispered in his ear in a soft voice, "Pretend to drink, but don't drink tonight." Giannetto understood her words, and went into the bed-chamber.

"You must be thirsty," said the lady, "and I want you to drink before you go to sleep."

And right away two damsels came in, looking like angels, with wine and sweetmeats according to the usual custom, and offered him drink.

"Who could refuse drink," said Giannetto, "seeing two such beautiful damsels?"

The lady laughed at that. And Giannetto took the cup and pretended to drink, but instead poured the wine into his bosom. The lady, believing him to have drunk, said to herself, "You will have to bring another ship, since you've just lost this one." Giannetto went to bed, feeling wide awake and in good spirits, and it seemed to him to take a thousand years for the lady to come to bed, and he said to himself, "For certain I've caught her this time; turnabout is fair play." To make the lady come to bed sooner, he began to snore and to feign sleep. "Everything is going fine," said the lady, and she quickly undressed and lay down by Giannetto. He lost no time: as soon as the lady was under the sheets, he turned toward her and embraced her and said, "Now I have what I have so much desired." And with these words he gave her the blissful peace that comes with holy matrimony, and all night long she did not leave his arms, so content was she. And next morning she arose before daylight and sent for all the barons and knights and other worthy citizens and said to them: "Giannetto is your lord; therefore make ready to celebrate." With that, a shout went up through all the land, "Long live our lord!" while bells and trumpets sounded. And she sent for many barons and counts from the surrounding countryside to come and see their lord. Then began a huge and splendid celebration. When Giannetto came out of the bedchamber, he was knighted and placed on the throne, and the scepter was put in his hand, and he was named lord with great ceremony and splendor. And as soon as all the barons and lords and ladies had come to court, he married the lady with such festivity and joy as can scarcely be told or imagined. All the lords and barons of the country came to the city to celebrate with jousts, trials of arms, dances, singing, the playing of instruments, and all that belongs to such a celebration. Signor Giannetto, like the generous and noble youth that he was, commenced to make gifts of silken materials and other rich things that he had brought with him. And he showed himself to be a strong ruler, one to be respected and feared, one who maintained right and justice on behalf of all sorts and conditions of men. And so he continued in joy and happiness, and took no thought or remem-

brance of poor Signor Ansaldo, who had pledged himself
for ten thousand florins to the Jew.

One day it happened that Signor Giannetto was at a window with his lady and saw pass through the square a company of men with torches in their hands who were going to
make an offering.

"What does that mean?" asked Signor Giannetto.

His lady answered, "That is a company of craftsmen, who
are going to make an offering at the Church of St. John,
whose festival is today."

At this Signor Giannetto remembered Signor Ansaldo. He
left the window, sighing deeply, his countenance changed,
and paced up and down the room several times thinking the
matter over. His wife asked him what was the matter.

"Nothing," he answered.

His wife began to question him, saying, "Something certainly is the matter with you, but you don't want to tell me."
And she kept asking so insistently that Signor Giannetto
told her the whole story, how Signor Ansaldo had pledged
himself for ten thousand florins, how the time for repay-
ment had expired this very day, and how Signor Ansaldo
would have to lose a pound of his flesh. His lady said to him,
"Quick, to horse, and take whatever company seems best to
you and a hundred thousand florins, and don't rest until
you are at Venice; and if he isn't dead yet, bring him back
here."

And so he at once ordered a trumpet to be sounded, and
mounted on horseback, with more than a hundred companions, and carrying enough money with him, he took his
leave and journeyed without delay toward Venice.

Now, it happened that with the arrival of the due date, the
Jew had Signor Ansaldo arrested and made clear his intention of taking a pound of flesh. Signor Ansaldo begged him
please to delay his death several days, so that if his Giannetto were to come, he would be able to see him.

"I am content to do what you wish as far as the delay is
concerned," said the Jew, "but even if he were to come a
hundred times, I intend to take a pound of flesh as specified
in the bond."

Signor Ansaldo answered that he was satisfied with this.
All Venice buzzed with this matter, and everyone was sorry
for Signor Ansaldo, and many merchants got together with

a view to paying the money, but the Jew would not agree to that, wishing instead to carry out the homicide so that he might say that he had put to death the greatest merchant in Christendom.

Now, it happened that when Signor Giannetto had set forth eagerly on his way, his lady had quickly followed after him, clad as a doctor of laws and taking two servants with her. Arriving in Venice, Signor Giannetto went to the house of the Jew, joyfully embraced Signor Ansaldo, and then said to the Jew that he was ready to pay him his money and as much more as he cared to demand. The Jew answered that he didn't want the money, since he had not received it on the date it was due, but that he wanted to take a pound of Signor Ansaldo's flesh. Over this matter there arose a great debate, and everyone blamed the Jew, but since Venice was a city that respected the rule of law and the Jew had his legal rights fully set forth and in the proper form, no one could find arguments to deny him; all they could do was plead with him. And so all the merchants of Venice came there to entreat the Jew, but he grew harder than ever. Signor Giannetto was willing to give him twenty thousand, and he refused that. He advanced his offer to thirty thousand, then forty, then fifty, and finally a hundred thousand florins.

The Jew said to him, "Do you want to know something? If you were to give me more than this whole city is worth, it would not satisfy me. I would rather have what the bond says is mine."

And that is where things stood in this dispute when, behold, the lady arrived in Venice, dressed like a doctor of laws, and alighted at an inn. The innkeeper asked one of the servants, "Who is this gentleman?"

The servant answered, "This gentleman is a doctor of laws coming from his studies at Bologna and returning home."

The innkeeper, hearing this, treated him with great respect. And while he was at the dinner table the doctor of laws said to the innkeeper, "How is this city of yours governed?"

"Sir," the innkeeper answered, "we make too much of justice here."

"How can that be?" said the doctor of laws.

"Sir," said the innkeeper, "I will tell you. Once there came here from Florence a young man called Giannetto, and he came here to his godfather, called Signor Ansaldo. He was so gracious and pleasing in his behavior that all the women, and the men too, were quite taken with him. Never before has there come to this city anyone so engaging as he. Now, this godfather of his fitted out for him, on three different occasions, three ships, all of the greatest value, and every time disaster struck. Signor Ansaldo didn't have enough money for the last ship, and so he borrowed ten thousand florins of a certain Jew on the condition that if he didn't repay what was due by St. John's Day in the following June, the said Jew would be authorized to take a pound of flesh from whatever part of him he pleased. Now this fortunate young man has come back and has offered to give, in place of those ten thousand florins, a hundred thousand, but the wicked Jew won't accept them. And all the good people of this place have been to him to plead with him, but to no avail."

"This is an easy question to settle," answered the doctor of laws.

"If you will only take the trouble to settle it," said the host, "so that this good man won't have to die, you will win the thanks and love of the worthiest young man that ever was born and of all the citizens of this land."

And so this doctor of laws had it proclaimed throughout the city that whoever had any legal question to settle should come to him. This was told to Signor Giannetto, that a doctor of laws had come from Bologna who was ready to settle any legal dispute.

Said Signor Giannetto to the Jew, "Let us go to this doctor of laws who I hear has arrived."

"All right, let us go," said the Jew.

When they came into the presence of the doctor of laws and offered him the respect that was his due, the doctor of laws at once recognized Signor Giannetto, but Signor Giannetto did not recognize him, because he had disguised his face with certain herbs. Signor Giannetto and the Jew stated their cases, each in turn and in proper order, before the doctor of laws.

The doctor of laws took the Jew's bond and read it, and then said to the Jew, "I would rather you took the hundred thousand florins and freed this good man, who will always be obliged to you."

"Nothing doing," said the Jew.

"It's your best course," said the doctor of laws.

The Jew said he absolutely refused.

"Now, come forward then," said the doctor of laws, "and take a pound of flesh from wherever you choose."

With that the Jew called for Signor Ansaldo. And when he had arrived, the doctor of laws said to the Jew, "Do your business." And so the Jew had him stripped naked and took in his hand a razor that he had prepared for the purpose and approached him from behind to seize him.

Signor Giannetto turned to the doctor of laws and said, "Sir, this is not what I asked you to do."

"Don't interfere," said the doctor of laws. "Let me handle this." And seeing that the Jew was about to start, the doctor of laws said, "Take care what you do. For if you take more or less than one pound, I will have your head struck off. And let me tell you, moreover, that if you shed a single drop of blood, I will have you put to death. Your bond makes no mention of the shedding of blood, but says only that you are to take a pound of flesh, neither more nor less. Now, if you are wise, you will think carefully what is the best way to do this." And then he at once had the executioner sent for and had him bring his block and ax, and said, "When I see a drop of blood flow, I will have your head struck off."

The Jew began to be afraid, and Signor Giannetto began to take heart. And after much argument, the Jew said, "Master Doctor, you are wiser than I am in these matters; let me be given those hundred thousand florins and I am content."

"I agree to your taking a pound of flesh," said the doctor of laws, "as your bond specifies; otherwise, I will not give you a penny. You should have taken it when I was willing to give it to you."

The Jew came down to ninety thousand, then eighty, but the doctor of laws held firm.

"Give him what he wants," said Signor Giannetto to the doctor of laws, "as long as he releases Signor Ansaldo."

"Let me handle this, I tell you," said the doctor of laws.

"Give me fifty thousand," said the Jew.

"I wouldn't give you the most miserable coin you've ever had," said the doctor of laws.

"Give me at least my ten thousand," said the Jew, "and a curse be on the air you breathe and the place where you live!"

"Didn't you hear what I said?" said the doctor of laws. "I won't give you a thing. If you want to take your forfeit from him, take it. If not, I will declare a nonperformance and void your bond."

Everyone present rejoiced greatly at this, and they all jeered at the Jew, saying, "He who thought to lay a trap has fallen into it himself." And so, seeing that he could not have his will, the Jew took his bond and tore it to pieces in a fury. Then Signor Ansaldo was freed and, with great rejoicing, was led home, and Signor Giannetto took those hundred thousand florins and went to the doctor of laws, finding him in his chambers making ready to depart.

Signor Giannetto went to him and said, "Sir, you have done me the greatest possible service, and for that reason I would like you to take home this money; you have well earned it."

"My dear Signor Giannetto," said the doctor of laws, "I thank you very much, but I have no need of it; take it yourself so that your lady won't be saying that you have spent it recklessly."

"By my faith," answered Signor Giannetto, "she is so generous and kind and good that even if I were to spend four times this, she would not mind; she asked if I wanted to bring much more than this."

"Are you happy with her?" said the doctor of laws.

"There is no creature in the world whom I love so dearly," answered Signor Giannetto, "for she is wise and beautiful, so much so that nature could do nothing more. And if you would do me the great favor of coming home to see her, you would marvel at the honorable reception she would give you, and you would see if she is all that I tell you."

"See to it, when you see her," said the doctor of laws, "that you greet her on my behalf."

"I shall do so," said Signor Giannetto, "but I wish you would take this money."

While he was saying this, the doctor of laws saw on his finger a ring, and so he said, "I would like that ring. I don't want any money."

"It shall be as you wish," said Signor Giannetto, "but I give it most unwillingly, since my wife gave it to me and said that I should wear it always for love of her; and if she sees me without it, she will think that I have given it to some woman and so be angry with me and believe that I am unfaithful; and the truth is that I love her more than I love myself."

"I am certain," answered the doctor of laws, "that she must love you well enough to believe you when you tell her that you have given it to me. But perhaps you want to give it to some former mistress of yours?"

"Such is the love and faith that I bear her," answered Signor Giannetto, "that there is no woman in the whole wide world for whom I would exchange her, so utterly beautiful is she in every way."

And thereupon he took the ring from his finger and gave it to the doctor of laws. Then they embraced and respectfully saluted each other and took their leave.

"Do me one favor," said the doctor of laws.

"You have only to ask," answered Signor Giannetto.

"Do not remain here," said the doctor of laws. "Go home quickly to see your wife."

"It seems to me a hundred thousand years," answered Signor Giannetto, "until I see her again."

And so they took their leave. The doctor of laws put out to sea, and with God's grace went on his journey. For his part Signor Giannetto gave banquets and made presents of horses and money to his friends, and thus made merry and kept open house, and then took his leave of all the Venetians, taking Signor Ansaldo with him; and many of his old friends went with them. And almost all the men and women of Venice were tearful at his departure, so graciously had he borne himself toward one and all the whole time that he had been in Venice. And so he left and returned to Belmont.

Now, it happened that his lady arrived some time before him and pretended she had been to the baths. She dressed herself as a woman, made festive preparations, had the streets hung in silk, and ordered many companies of soldiers to array themselves. When Signor Giannetto and

Signor Ansaldo arrived, all the barons and the court went to greet them, shouting, "Long live our lord! Long live our lord!" And when they arrived at the city, the lady ran to embrace Signor Ansaldo but pretended to be a little angry with Signor Giannetto, even though she loved him better than herself. A great celebration was made, with jousting, feats of arms, and dancing and singing by all the barons and ladies and damsels who were there. But Signor Giannetto, seeing that his wife did not receive him with her accustomed kindness, went to their room and called her, and said, "What's wrong?" and tried to embrace her.

"There's no need here for these embraces," said the lady, "for I know only too well that you have been meeting your former mistresses."

Signor Giannetto started to deny this.

"Where is the ring I gave you?" said his lady.

"What I thought would happen has indeed happened," said Signor Giannetto. "I said you would think badly of me. But I swear by the faith I bear to God and to you that I gave that ring to the doctor of laws who brought me victory in the case."

"And I swear by the faith I bear to God and to you," said his lady, "that you gave it to a woman. I know it, and aren't you ashamed to swear as you have sworn?"

"May God wipe me from the face of the earth," said Signor Giannetto, "if I am not speaking true, and if I did not say to that doctor of laws as I have told you, when he asked for the ring."

"You should have stayed in Venice," said his lady, "and sent Signor Ansaldo here while you enjoyed yourself with your mistresses, who, I hear, were all in tears when you left."

Then Signor Giannetto began to weep and to give himself over to grief, saying, "You are swearing what isn't true and couldn't possibly be true."

When his lady saw him weeping, it seemed to her like a knife wound to the heart, and at once she ran and embraced him, laughing heartily; and she showed him the ring and told him everything—what he had said to the doctor of laws, how she herself was that doctor of laws. Signor Giannetto was greatly astonished at this and, seeing that it was all true, was immensely amused. He went out of the room and told the story to some of his barons and friends. And this adventure increased and multiplied the love between the couple. Then Signor Giannetto summoned the maid-servant who had warned him that evening not to drink, and gave her in marriage to Signor Ansaldo. And so they lived ever after in happiness and pleasure, and enjoyed good things and good fortune.

Il Pecorone by Ser Giovanni Fiorentino was first published in Milan in 1558. This new translation is based on the critical edition prepared under the supervision of Enzo Esposito, Longo Editore, Ravenna, 1974, which was based in turn on manuscript sources as well as the early printed texts.

Further Reading

Auden, W. H. "Brothers and Others." *"The Dyer's Hand" and Other Essays*. New York: Random House, 1948. In a casual but seminal essay on the play, Auden calls *The Merchant of Venice* one of Shakespeare's "Unpleasant Plays." The presence of Antonio and Shylock disrupts the unambiguous fairy-tale world of romantic comedy, reminding us that the utopian qualities of Belmont are illusory: "in the real world, no hatred is totally without justification, no love totally innocent."

Barber, C. L. "The Merchants and the Jew of Venice: Wealth's Communion and an Intrude." *Shakespeare's Festive Comedy*. Princeton, N.J.: Princeton-Univ. Press, 1959. Barber acknowledges that while *"on reflection"* Shakespeare's handling of the use of wealth and his depiction of Shylock are disturbing, in the theater the play's insistent festive design works to affirm "its concern for the grace of community." As a threat to the social harmony that the comedy celebrates, Shylock, "who embodies the evil side of the power of money," must be removed.

Barnet, Sylvan, ed. *Twentieth Century Interpretations of "The Merchant of Venice."* Englewood Cliffs, N.J.: Prentice-Hall, 1970. To help modern students see the play as Elizabethans would have, Barnet provides a useful collection of interpretive and historical essays, including studies by Auden, Barber, Granville-Barker, Kermode, and Moody that are discussed here.

Brown, John Russell. "The Realization of Shylock: A Theatrical Criticism." In *Early Shakespeare*, ed. John Russell Brown and Bernard Harris. Stratford-upon-Avon Studies 3. London: Edward Arnold, 1961. Brown argues that Shylock dominates the stage and that the meaning of the character can fully be discovered only in performance. He examines the "opportunities given to the actor by Shakespeare" and the acting traditions established by Charles Macklin, Edmund Kean, Henry Irving, and Sir John Gielgud.

Burckhardt, Sigurd. "*The Merchant of Venice:* The Gentle Bond." *ELH* 29 (1962): 239–262. Rpt. in *Shakespearean Meanings*. Princeton, N.J.: Princeton Univ. Press, 1968. Burckhardt identifies "the bond" as the play's controlling metaphor and explores the way attention to it reveals the play's exacting structure. The comic design of the play, Burckhardt argues, emerges when "the vicious circle of the bond's law" is "transformed into the ring of love."

Cohen, D. M. "The Jew and Shylock." *Shakespeare Quarterly* 31 (1980): 53–63. In spite of its many defenders, the play, for Cohen, remains profoundly anti-Semitic. Shylock's humanity is effaced and his Jewishness used to alienate him from the world of the play and the audience. "It is as though," Cohen writes, "*The Merchant of Venice* is an anti-Semitic play written by an author who is not an anti-Semite—but an author who has been willing to use the cruel stereotypes of that ideology for mercenary and artistic purposes."

Danson, Lawrence. *The Harmonies of "The Merchant of Venice."* New Haven, Conn.: Yale Univ. Press, 1978. As his title reveals, Danson is concerned with the play's "harmonies" rather than the discordant notes heard by many modern critics. He sensitively explores a series of dramatic oppositions that are posed but finally resolved by the play: law/freedom, justice/mercy, feuding/marriage, Jew/Christian, Venice/Belmont.

Evans, Bertrand. *Shakespeare's Comedies.* Esp. pp. 46–67. Oxford: Clarendon Press, 1960. The comic design of *The Merchant of Venice*, Evans finds, is determined by the manipulation of discrepancies of awareness between characters and the audience of the play. Only when these discrepancies dissolve in the trial scene, with the revelation of Portia's remarkable control of events, can we be confident that "the world of *The Merchant of Venice* is one in which goodness and mirth prevail," and only then can we experience any sympathy for Shylock.

Girard, René. "'To Entrap the Wisest': A Reading of *The Merchant of Venice.*" In *Literature and Society: Selected Papers from the English Institute, 1978*, ed. Edward W. Said. Baltimore and London: The Johns Hopkins Univ. Press, 1980. Girard explores the disturbing symmetries that the play establishes between Jew and Christian.

Their mutual hatred, according to Girard, turns Shylock and Antonio into "doubles of each other," creating a moral burden for an audience confronted with action that simultaneously produces and undermines the scapegoating of Shylock.

Granville-Barker, Harley. *"The Merchant of Venice."* In *Prefaces to Shakespeare*, vol. 4, 1946. Rpt. Princeton, N.J.: Princeton Univ. Press, 1966. With his characteristic sensitivity to the demands of performance, Granville-Barker examines the play's form and temper. For him, *"The Merchant of Venice* is the simplest of plays, so long as we do not bedevil it with sophistries": the "unlikelihood" of its fairy-tale plot is "redeemed by veracity of character."

Kermode, Frank. "The Mature Comedies." In *Early Shakespeare*, ed. John Russell Brown and Bernard Harris. Stratford-upon-Avon Studies 3. London: Edward Arnold, 1961. In his account of Shakespeare's mature comic vision, Kermode finds *The Merchant of Venice* designed around a contrast between "gentleness" and "its opposite, for which Shylock stands." The comedy, Kermode says, confirms Christian values and patterns: it begins with "usury and corrupt love" and moves purposefully toward "harmony and perfect love."

Leggatt, Alexander. *"The Merchant of Venice." Shakespeare's Comedy of Love*. New York: Barnes and Noble, 1974. Leggatt explores the tension the play generates between its formalized and conventional plot and its characters' "human reality, naturalistically conceived." The formal design moves toward harmony and happiness but can have, Leggatt argues, "only a limited success in bringing order out of an intractable world."

Moody, A. D. *Shakespeare: "The Merchant of Venice."* London: Edward Arnold, 1964. In this short book (64 pages), Moody argues that the play presents a deeply ironic portrait of the Christian community. It reveals the essential "likeness" of Shylock and his accusers and "does not celebrate the Christian virtues so much as expose their absence."

Nevo, Ruth. "Jessica's Monkey; or, the Goodwins." *Comic Transformations in Shakespeare*. London and New York: Methuen, 1980. Nevo explores "the rupture of comic form" in the play, which never fully credits either the idealizations of Belmont or the scapegoating of Venice. The play, Nevo finds, takes its power precisely from this refusal to resolve the dichotomies it poses.

Palmer, D. J. *"The Merchant of Venice,* or the Importance of Being Earnest." In *Shakespearian Comedy,* ed. Malcolm Bradbury and D. J. Palmer. Stratford-upon-Avon Studies 14. London: Edward Arnold, 1972. Palmer recognizes the powerful discords of the play and its prevailing seriousness. Antonio's sadness at the opening of the play, Palmer finds, "sets in motion the forces of division and disharmony which will take the play to the brink of tragedy before it is retrieved as a comedy."

Rabkin, Norman. "Meaning and *The Merchant of Venice." Shakespeare and the Problem of Meaning.* Chicago: Univ. of Chicago Press, 1981. As part of an argument about the limitation of "meaning as the principle of unity in a work," Rabkin explores the tensions, contradictions, and ambivalent signals that the play generates. The structure of the play, Rabkin finds, demands from an audience a constant reassessment of what it has seen, presenting it with elements "provocative of inconsistent responses."

Stoll, E. E. "Shylock." *Journal of English and Germanic Philology* 10 (1911): 236–279. Rpt. in *Shakespeare Studies: Historical and Comparative in Method.* New York: Macmillan, 1927. Stoll denies that Shylock is presented sympathetically; rather, he is a conventional, comic stage villain who exists to be foiled. From an analysis of the literary and cultural traditions underlying the character, Stoll concludes that our "notions of justice and social responsibility" distort the play's "intention."

Memorable Lines

Your mind is tossing on the ocean.   (SALERIO 1.1.8)

You have too much respect upon the world;
They lose it that do buy it with much care.

                    (GRATIANO 1.1.74–75)

I hold the world but as the world, Gratiano,
A stage where every man must play a part,
And mine a sad one.   (ANTONIO 1.1.77–79)

Let me play the fool!   (GRATIANO 1.1.79)

  "I am Sir Oracle,
And when I ope my lips let no dog bark!"

                    (GRATIANO 1.1.93–94)

They are as sick that surfeit with too much as they that
starve with nothing.   (NERISSA 1.2.5–6)

God made him, and therefore let him pass for a man.

                    (PORTIA 1.2.54–55)

When he is best he is a little worse than a man, and when he
is worst he is little better than a beast.   (PORTIA 1.2.86–87)

I will buy with you, sell with you, talk with you, walk with
you, and so following, but I will not eat with you, drink with
you, nor pray with you.   (SHYLOCK 1.3.33–35)

What news on the Rialto?   (SHYLOCK 1.3.35–36)

The devil can cite Scripture for his purpose.

                    (ANTONIO 1.3.96)

It is a wise father that knows his own child.

                    (LAUNCELOT 2.2.73–74)

But love is blind, and lovers cannot see
The pretty follies that themselves commit.

(JESSICA   2.6.37–38)

"Who chooseth me must give and hazard all he hath."

(Inscription   2.7.9)

"My daughter! O, my ducats! O, my daughter!"

(SOLANIO parodying Shylock   2.8.15)

I am a Jew. Hath not a Jew eyes? Hath not a Jew hands, organs, dimensions, senses, affections, passions?

(SHYLOCK   3.1.55–57)

If you prick us, do we not bleed? If you tickle us, do we not laugh? If you poison us, do we not die? And if you wrong us, shall we not revenge?

(SHYLOCK   3.1.60–63)

Tell me where is fancy bred,
Or in the heart or in the head?
How begot, how nourishèd?
   Reply, reply.

(Song   3.2.63–66)

The world is still deceived with ornament.

(BASSANIO   3.2.74)

"I never knew so young a body with so old a head."

(Letter   4.1.162–163)

The quality of mercy is not strained.
It droppeth as the gentle rain from heaven
Upon the place beneath. It is twice blest:
It blesseth him that gives and him that takes.

(PORTIA   4.1.182–185)

And earthly power doth then show likest God's
When mercy seasons justice.

(PORTIA   4.1.194–195)

He is well paid that is well satisfied.

(PORTIA   4.1.413)

The moon shines bright. In such a night as this . . .

(LORENZO   5.1.1)

How sweet the moonlight sleeps upon this bank!
(LORENZO   5.1.54)

   Look how the floor of heaven
Is thick inlaid with patens of bright gold.
(LORENZO   5.1.58–59)

There's not the smallest orb which thou behold'st
But in his motion like an angel sings,
Still choiring to the young-eyed cherubins.
(LORENZO   5.1.60–62)

The man that hath no music in himself,
Nor is not moved with concord of sweet sounds,
Is fit for treasons, stratagems, and spoils.
(LORENZO   5.1.83–85)

How far that little candle throws his beams!
So shines a good deed in a naughty world.
(PORTIA   5.1.90–91)

The crow doth sing as sweetly as the lark
When neither is attended.   (PORTIA   5.1.102–103)

Contributors

DAVID BEVINGTON, Phyllis Fay Horton Professor of Humanities at the University of Chicago, is editor of *The Complete Works of Shakespeare* (Scott, Foresman, 1980) and of *Medieval Drama* (Houghton Mifflin, 1975). His latest critical study is *Action Is Eloquence: Shakespeare's Language of Gesture* (Harvard University Press, 1984).

DAVID SCOTT KASTAN, Professor of English and Comparative Literature at Columbia University, is the author of *Shakespeare and the Shapes of Time* (University Press of New England, 1982).

JAMES HAMMERSMITH, Associate Professor of English at Auburn University, has published essays on various facets of Renaissance drama, including literary criticism, textual criticism, and printing history.

ROBERT KEAN TURNER, Professor of English at the University of Wisconsin–Milwaukee, is a general editor of the New Variorum Shakespeare (Modern Language Association of America) and a contributing editor to *The Dramatic Works in the Beaumont and Fletcher Canon* (Cambridge University Press, 1966–).

JAMES SHAPIRO, who coedited the bibliographies with David Scott Kastan, is Assistant Professor of English at Columbia University.

✣

JOSEPH PAPP, one of the most important forces in theater today, is the founder and producer of the New York Shakespeare Festival, America's largest and most prolific theatrical institution. Since 1954 Mr. Papp has produced or directed all but one of Shakespeare's plays—in Central Park, in schools, off and on Broadway, and at the Festival's permanent home, The Public Theater. He has also produced such award-winning plays and musical works as *Hair, A Chorus Line, Plenty,* and *The Mystery of Edwin Drood,* among many others.

THE COMPLETE WORKS IN 29 VOLUMES
Edited, with introductions by David Bevington
•Forewords by Joseph Papp

Bantam Books, Dept. SH2, 2451 South Wolf Road, Des Plaines, IL 60018

Please send me the items I have checked above. I am enclosing $_____ (please add $2.50 to cover postage and handling). Send check or money order, no cash or C.O.D.s please.

Mr/Ms _____

Address _____

City/State _____ Zip _____

SH2–3/92

Please allow four to six weeks for delivery.
Prices and availability subject to change without notice.

DISCOVER
THE DRAMA OF LIFE
IN THE LIFE OF DRAMA

☐	26366-8	**THE ACTOR'S SCENEBOOK** by M. Schulman & E. Mekler	$5.95
☐	26581-4	**THE ACTOR'S SCENEBOOK II** by M. Schulman & E. Mekler	$4.95
☐	25434-0	**FILM SCENES FOR ACTORS** Joshua Karton	$4.95
☐	26804-X	**FILM SCENES FOR ACTORS II** Joshua Karton	$5.95
☐	21280-X	**FOUR GREAT PLAYS** Henrik Ibsen	$3.50
☐	25844-3	**MODERN AMERICAN SCENES** **FOR STUDENT ACTORS** Wynn Handman	$4.50
☐	34611-3	**SAM SHEPARD: SEVEN PLAYS** Sam Shepard (Large Format)	$10.00
☐	27838-X	**THE NIGHT THOREAU SPENT IN JAIL** Jerome Lawrence and Robert E. Lee	$3.95
☐	26618-7	**BRIAN'S SONG** William Blinn	$3.99
☐	28028-7	**THE EFFECTS OF GAMMA RAYS** **ON MAN-IN-THE-MOON MARIGOLDS** Paul Zindel	$3.95
☐	26915-1	**INHERIT THE WIND** Lawrence & Lee	$3.99
☐	21363-6	**EURIPIDES Ten Plays** Moses Hadas, ed.	$4.95
☐	24778-6	**THE MIRACLE WORKER** William Gibson	$3.50
☐	34932-5	**THE TECHNIQUE OF** **ACTING** Stella Adler	$10.00
☐	34590-7	**FOOL FOR LOVE AND** **OTHER PLAYS** Sam Shepard	$10.00

Buy them at your local bookstore or use this page to order.

Bantam Books, Dept. EDH, 2351 South Wolf Road, Des Plaines, IL 60018

Please send me the items I have checked above. I am enclosing $_____
(please add $2.50 to cover postage and handling). Send check or money
order, no cash or C.O.D.s please.

Mr/Ms _____

Address _____

City/State _____ Zip _____

EDH–6/92

Please allow four to six weeks for delivery.
Prices and availability subject to change without notice.

By the year 2000, 2 out of 3 Americans could be illiterate.

It's true.

Today, 75 million adults... about one American in three, can't read adequately. And by the year 2000, U.S. News & World Report envisions an America with a literacy rate of only 30%.

Before that America comes to be, you can stop it... by joining the fight against illiteracy today.

Call the Coalition for Literacy at toll-free **1-800-228-8813** and volunteer.

Volunteer Against Illiteracy. The only degree you need is a degree of caring.

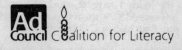

Ad Council Coalition for Literacy

LWA